THE EXPERT WITNESS SURVIVAL MANUAL

THE EXPERT WITNESS SURVIVAL MANUAL

By

FRANK J. MACHOVEC, PH.D., A.B.P.H.

AN AUTHORS GUILD BACKINPRINT.COM EDITION

iUniverse, Inc.
Bloomington

THE EXPERT WITNESS SURVIVAL MANUAL

AN AUTHORS GUILD BACKINPRINT.COM EDITION

Published by iUniverse, Inc.

For information address:
iUniverse
1663 Liberty Drive
Bloomington, IN 47403
www.iuniverse.com
1-800-Authors (1-800-288-4677)

Originally published by Charles C Thomas • Publisher

ISBN: 978-1-4759-6011-2 (sc)

Printed in the United States of America

iUniverse rev. date: 11/29/2012

ABOUT THE AUTHOR

FRANK MACHOVEC is a psychologist who has testified as an expert witness in civil and criminal court cases and administrative, investigative and legislative hearings in the Unived States and Canada since 1975. He regularly speaks to professional associations on matters of ethics and law—most recently at the First and Third National Conferences on Post Traumatic Stress Disorder on use of that disorder as a legal defense; risk management in the use of hypnosis at state and national conferences; and "courtroom survival" for school psychologists at Kent State University.

Doctor MacHovec conducts special training programs and workshops to help prepare expert witnesses to testify. His courtroom coping techniques have been published in **Communique**, the national newsletter of the National Association of School Psychologists, and articles on risk management aspects of professional practice appear regularly in scientific journals. The enthusiastic response to them and to his training workshops stimulated the writing of this book.

Doctor MacHovec holds many professional memberships; those most relevant to courtroom work are: American College of Forensic Psychology; Society for Personality Assessment; American Board of Medical Psychotherapists; and the American Association for Marital and Family Therapy. In 1982, Division 18 of the American Psychological Association (Psychologists in Public Service) awarded him a National Certificate of Recognition for his field work on ethical standards for hypnosis.

His forensic experience began in Canada in 1975 and continued in the United States. He has served as chief psychologist in community mental health clinics and mental hospitals and was a clinical psychologist on a medium-security unit for the mentally ill convicted of felonies.

To truth, justice and law;
may they always coexist

PREFACE

THIS IS NOT a book for lawyers. They already know the contents from their education and experience. It is not for experienced expert witnesses. They also know the contents from the acid test of actively participating in the legal process. Rather, it is "a survival manual" for those who have never testified before or who do so infrequently.

I have been an expert witness in a variety of courts—high and low—and at formal and informal hearings in the United States and Canada since the early 1970s. When I began, there were no books such as this to explain the legal process in simple terms, point out potential pitfalls, and help the expert new to court to prepare, psychologically as well as professionally.

Court can be like a pleasant dream or it can be a nightmare. I learned the hard way, in "courtroom combat," a solitary and painful experience. It is hoped this book will serve as an "inoculation" against the emotional distress many first-time witnesses suffer. There is the stress of seemingly unending hours of apprehension waiting for the day to testify, then a seeming eternity while sequestered alone waiting in a witness room. There is the infantile fear that the opposing attorney is the Devil, the judge is God, and **both** are out to get you, while the attorney who requested your testimony sits back, feet on the desk, reading the paper while you testify, are verbally attacked, die and are buried in an unmarked grave without benefit of clergy. That's how it feels for many of us.

I've tried to keep the language simple, the style light, and at the same time provide a comprehensive overview of expert witness testimony and also the legal process and the usual trial procedures. The Glossary defines the most used legal terms and concepts and can be a minicourse in "legalese." I suggest you take this book with you and read it or skim through it while you wait to testify. May it serve you as a reassuring friend whose presence lessens tension and anxiety. Law firms may find this book useful to loan out to expert witnesses and consultants to help them prepare. It could save much time and provide a good working knowledge of legal process.

Two words of caution: First, laws and legal procedures vary from state to state, state to federal courts, and there can also be variations as agreed in trial procedure because of the uniqueness of the case. In South Carolina, attorneys stand in court to speak. In Virginia they need not stand to address the court. Expert witnesses should consult with the attorney who has requested their testimony about specific legal procedures required. Second, no book is a substitute for legal advice "live" from an attorney. Expert witnesses must rely on the knowledge and judgment of the attorneys with whom they are working. I am not an attorney and defer to judges, attorneys and other officers of the court to further clarify and explain to prospective witnesses the content of this book as it pertains to the case at hand.

Frank J. MacHovec, Ph.D.
Director
Center for the Study of the Self
3804 Hawthorne Avenue
Richmond, Virginia 23222

ACKNOWLEDGMENTS

OF THE MANY sources of information used to write this book, by far the most helpful was actually testifying in courts and at hearings, the experience there with defendants and plaintiffs, their attorneys, other expert witnesses friendly and opposing, judges and juries, other court officers, and newspaper and media representatives.

Though judges officially qualify expert witnesses, attorneys first choose them, and to be asked more than once by the same attorney has been for me a special privilege. I acknowledge their trust and confidence and want them to know the feeling is mutual. My thanks to them, especially those with whom I have worked during the preparation of this book: Ron Williams, Ted Huggins, John Heard and Bob Whitt.

Last but not least, the Information Services Office of the American Bar Association provided law journal reprints and other valuable background material which added to and enriched this book. Their service to me was prompt, professional and the material always relevant and meaningful.

CONTENTS

Page

Preface ix

Chapter 1. Expert Witnesses: Who, What, Why? 3

Current status, scope and applications; who is qualified? What is expected? Types of courts, federal and state; types of law; types of trials; typical civil and criminal proceedings; references.

Chapter 2. Law as Idea and Ideal 17

Historical and philosophical heritage of natural and moral law; ancient civilizations: Hammurabi; Sumer; Golden Age of Greece; Old Testament; Roman Law; in modern European history; early American history; theory and practice; references.

Chapter 3. Law: The Realities 33

Practice vs. principle; the adversary system; court as drama; as it happens (court chronology); pretrial phase; trial phase; references.

Chapter 4. Lawyering 51

Law and science; lawyer jokes; the rise of the legal profession; lawyering today; lawyer types and techniques, good and bad; Abe Lincoln, prairie lawyer; references.

Chapter 5. Expert Witness Practice Details 73

Hired gun or village blacksmith; selecting experts; comparative credibility; 12 virtues of the ideal expert witness; qualifying; discoverability; interrogatories; depositions; initial contact with attorney; engagement letter; subpoenas; court orders; conflicting testimony; testimony as idea and ideal; using a law library; references.

Chapter 6. Coping and Survival 99

Law as a word world; physical preparation; mental preparation; planning; performance tips; survival tactics; conclusions; references.

Glossary 121
Author Index 161
Subject Index 163
Quick Reference Tactics Index 169

THE EXPERT WITNESS SURVIVAL MANUAL

CHAPTER 1

EXPERT WITNESSES: WHO, WHAT, WHY?

Experto credite
("believe an expert")
Virgil (70-19 B.C.)
The Aeneid, XI, 283

THE GROWING use of expert witnesses in courts throughout the nation has been described as "a boom town phenomenon" and a "new growth industry." Ads offering expert witness testimony and consultation are regularly published in law journals and in mailings to trial lawyers. At the 1983 midwinter conference of the American Trial Lawyers Association, Mary Fran Edwards referred to the increase in expert witness testimony as "one of the country's newest growth industries . . . the result of the litigation system responding to a more technical world . . . the increasing complexity of society" (**American Bar Association Journal,** 1983, p. 429).

The rise in expert witness testimony is also a by-product of a variety of other factors. There has been an increase in the number of lawsuits filed. As many social commentators have observed, we appear to be "a litigious society." Anybody can sue for almost any reason—and do. Morgan (1987) reported that in 1985 a lawsuit was filed at a per capita ratio of one for every fifteen Americans. In 1966 there were 70,906 lawsuits filed in federal courts; in 1986 there were 254,828 (Kester, 1987). There were 401 verdicts exceeding $1 million each for medical malpractice in 1984. By 1985 the average medical malpractice award was $1 million. In Virginia, one malpractice case resulted in an $8 million verdict upheld later by a federal appeals court, though the nationwide record may be the verdict of over $15 million. In the 10-year period from 1974 to 1984 there was a 600 percent increase in product liability awards, from an average of $1,579 in 1974 to an average of $10,745 in 1984. Studies by the Rand Corporation indicate most cases are settled on appeal at half the damages initially awarded.

There is also a rise in claims based on "psychic harm" from a wide range of alleged causes such as witnessing a crime, contagious diseases (e.g. AIDS, staphylococcus infections), accidents and negligence, toxic substances (e.g. Agent Orange, asbestos, radon, formaldehyde fumes, mercury in fish, oil spills at sea, polluted water, insecticides), defective products even when properly used (e.g. appliances, toys, automobiles), and "acts of God" (e.g. floods, earthquakes).

Damage suits are sometimes filed charging several defendants, directly or only indirectly involved or at best marginally at fault, so that the plaintiff, if successful, can be paid by whomever has insurance coverage or assets, the so-called **deep pockets** approach. Suing for some is like buying a ticket to a lottery—but with better odds. With the right ticket you can win big, from whomever has money. There's a good chance you won't have to go to court to collect: "Many people with even a frivolous grievance or injury consider a lawsuit knowing that insurance companies will be likely to settle out of court to avoid high defense costs" (Morgan, 1987, p. 11).

EXPERT WITNESSES: WHO, WHAT, WHERE?

Expert witnesses can be anyone with special skills or knowledge which surpasses the average person and which is needed by the court to determine legal truth. The expert can be a cosmetologist or college professor, barber or banker, professional or technician or an experienced factory worker. **Black's Law Dictionary** (1979) defines expert witnesses as "persons qualified to speak authoritatively by reason of their special training, skill, or familiarity with the subject" or "evidence of persons who are skilled in some art, science, profession or business, which skill or knowledge is not common to their fellow men and which has come . . . by reason of special study and experience . . . ." **Federal Rules of Evidence 702 and 703** state that if "scientific, technology or other specialized knowledge will assist the trier of fact to understand the evidence or to determine a fact in issue, a witness qualified as an expert by knowledge, skill, experience, training or education may testify thereto in the form of an opinion or otherwise." The key factor differentiating expert witnesses from others is the legal privilege of expressing an **opinion.** Other witnesses testify only to **facts,** what they witnessed firsthand, what they saw, did or said. They are therefore called **fact witnesses.**

Case law in different states offers a variety of definitions of an expert witness, but all are quite similar in content. Here's a sampling: "opinion evidence of some person who possesses special skill or knowledge in some science, profession or business which is not common to the average man . . . by reason of special study or experience" **(Bd of Ed Claymont Special Sch Dist v. 13 Acres Brandywine, Del. Super., 11 Terry 387, 131 A.2d 180, 184).** A person who "by habits of life and business has peculiar skill in forming opinion on a subject in dispute" (**Brown v. State, 140 Ga.App. 160, 230 S.E.2d 128, 131).** "One who by reason of education or specialized experience possesses a superior knowledge respecting a subject about which persons having no particular training are incapable of forming an accurate opinion or deducing correct conclusions" (**Kim Mfg v. Superior Metal Treating, Mo.App., 537 S.W.2d 424, 428).** These definitions are excerpted from **Black's Law Dictionary,** 1979, p. 519.

There are firms specializing in locating local or out-of-state experts to help attorneys more effectively present their cases. One such organization boasts 6,000 experts in 3,000 subject areas. Another advertises 2,000 "board-certified medical experts in all specialties." Historically, experts have been researchers, scientists, college professors, engineers and medical and mental health professionals testifying on product liability, malpractice or mental competence. Today, however, there are an even greater variety of experts and the types of cases in which their knowledge and skills are applied. There are experts on "weather, railroad air brakes, bicycles, tire mounting, lawn mowers, swimming pools, handwriting, fires and explosions, ballistics, elevators and escalators, police conduct and just about anything else that might be the subject of dispute" (**American Bar Association Journal,** 1983, p. 429). A recent issue of a national lawyers' newsletter contained ads for expert witnesses in addiction and DWI defense, jail malpractice, hot air balloon accidents and warning labels and "toxic torts."

WHAT TESTIMONY AND WHY?

Expert witnesses and expert consultants provide lawyers, judges and juries with specialized information in the form of a professional, carefully considered opinion needed and not otherwise available. Expert testimony fills a very real need in today's legal justice system which increasingly deals with very complex subjects. Hess (1985) observed that "the breaking up of AT&T was based on a judge spending a decade reading more material than would fill a railway car" (p. 75). Typically, experts analyze and interpret facts and inform the court as to how science or technology would approach a real or hypothetical situation. More specialized applications of expert witness testimony are: estimating mortality or longevity in wrongful death cases; earning potential if uninjured; product, safety or design standards; breach of warranty; copyright, trademark or patent infringement; optimal industry standards; and in health and psychiatric settings, standards of care as opposed to alleged negligence or malpractice.

Experts are testifying daily in state and federal courts and hearings throughout the land, in such cases as: child custody (best interest of the child) sometimes involving a gay parent or couple, grandparent rights or religious cults and communes; malpractice and negligence to help determine liability for wrongful death, permanent or temporary disability; forensic (criminal) cases to assess competence to stand trial or at the time of the offense; personal injury; and product defects. They testify, too, in a variety of informal and formal hearings: regulatory (e.g. rate setting); legislative (state legislature, congressional, senate); administrative (e.g. social security disability appeals), investigative (e.g. grand jury) and criminal sentencing to recommend prison or probation.

Once qualified, experts have the same sworn duty as all witnesses: "To tell the truth, the whole truth and nothing but the truth, so help you God." But unlike other witnesses which are also called "fact witnesses," experts are entitled and expected to have an opinion on some important aspect of the case. This distinguishes the expert from all other witnesses. It also burdens the expert with the duty and obligation to remain objective. Cicero (106-43 B.C.) could have spoken to today's expert witnesses when he wrote these three rules for historians: "The first law is never to dare utter an untruth. The second is to suppress nothing that is true. Moreover, there should be no partiality or malice . . ." (**De Oratore,** II, 62).

Expert witnesses have a right to be heard because of the nature of their function and the court's need for information which only they possess. While rules of evidence vary from state to state and state to federal courts, most follow the intent of **Rule 702** of the **Federal Rules of Evidence** that those with "knowledge, skill, experience, training or education" can be called upon to testify when there is a need for specialized information which only they have. Ostroff (1982) points out that "an expert need not even have complete knowledge of his field of expertise to be certain of his opinion" (p. 8).

This is not always a simple task. In **Frye v. U. S., 293 F. 1013 (D.C. Cir. 1923)** the court in its decision pointed out the "twilight zone" that can exist between fact and deduction and the need to sharpen the focus between them:

> The line between the experimental and demonstrable stages . . . is a twilight zone. While courts will go a long way in admitting expert testimony deduced from a well recognized scientific principle or discovery, the thing from which the deduction is made must be sufficiently established to have gained general acceptance in the particular field in which it belongs.

Experts take the standard, traditional witnesses' oath to tell the truth and the added obligation to inform the court as needed on subjects within their area of expertise. That does not mean the expert's opinion will be eagerly accepted, without resistance or even open hostility. First and foremost, the trial process is an adversarial system of polar opposite positions. Attorneys on both sides will try to the best of their abilities to use an expert's testimony, whatever it is, to further their own case. This is their sworn duty as advocates for their clients, and sometimes they pursue this goal with what seems an "end-justifies-the-means" attitude and style which can cut into an expert witness's self-esteem and self-confidence.

In "the heat of battle" while "under fire" on the witness stand, it can be very difficult to retain composure and "stick to your guns." Law is a word world and lawyers are skilled in the use of words, their meaning, interpretation and application to legal standards and requirements. Expert witnesses must exert special care in what they choose to write in reports and evaluations submitted in evidence and what they say in testimony and what they do while testifying. Doing so is much like holding a boat or airplane on course in a storm.

The foregoing paragraphs describe several facets or factors of expert witness testimony. For some experts, testifying is a business, a career. They do little else. They are listed in witness registries and some have titles such as diplomates in forensic psychiatry or forensic psychology, based on postgraduate written and oral examinations. For other experts, testifying can be a harrowing, humiliating, painful experience second only to torture in a dungeon cell by a crazed sadist or the unceasing interrogation in a James Bond movie. Still other experts find testifying a "battle of wits," verbal combat, sparring with an adversary like a spirited game or sport. It can be all these and the more you testify, the more likely you will experience every one of these factors.

There is a deeper, more meaningful aspect of expert testimony. To be accepted as a person with the knowledge and skills a court needs is a special privilege. To be allowed and expected to have and give an opinion within your own unique area of expertise is an honor, a distinction. To "tell it like it is," state the truth, and hold fast to it despite whatever opposing attorneys say and do is a duty not much different than a police officer who swears "to uphold the law" or for that matter a soldier who swears to "defend the nation." In these ways, experts share a deep and honorable calling, those who render a service to the highest ideals of the country.

John Stuart Mill (1806-1873), the English philosopher, economist, writer and proponent of women's rights, described two "lamentable transactions" of "judicial iniquity" from history—the conviction and execution of Socrates and Jesus. Neither had the benefit of equal legal counsel to the opposition. There were no expert witnesses in either court. "There was once a man named Socrates," Mill wrote, an "acknowledged master of all the eminent thinkers who have since lived, whose fame still grows after more than 2,000 years . . . was put to death by his countrymen after a judicial conviction, for impiety and immorality." Mill defines the grounds: "impiety in denying the gods recognized by the State . . . immorality in being . . . by his instructions a 'corruptor of youth' " (Webb, 1951, p. 111).

Mill then considered the plight of Jesus who stood silently before Pilate, making no plea: "the only other instance of judicial iniquity . . . the event which took place on Calvary." It is interesting to note that this incident in legend and history is the basis for a "not guilty" plea recorded for a defendant who stands mute when asked to plead. Mill concludes: "These men were, to all appearance, not bad men, not worse than men commonly are but rather the contrary, men who possessed in a full or somewhat more than a full measure of religious, moral and patriotic feelings . . . the very kind of men who in all times, our own included, should have every chance of passing through life blameless and respected" (ibid.).

Would expert witnesses in those two tragic cases have made a difference? If John Stuart Mill had been the expert, the verdicts may have been different. What if you were the expert in those trials? You may feel unequal to such a task now, but it is hoped that reading this book will help you bolster your self-confidence and feel more comfortable with your competence. You **can** make a difference in court, just for being there, for the information you alone can provide above and beyond obstacles set in your path by the most energetic opposing attorney.

TYPES OF COURTS

The court system in the United States was established by the **Constitution,** a product of the sociopolitical awakening and activism of the American Revolution. Prior to it, there were French, Spanish and English courts in the colonies founded by those three competing nations. Even after the **Constitution,** "frontier justice" hanged horse thieves and bank robbers until cities grew and the local populace insisted on more civilized due process. There is a dual system of federal and state courts.

FEDERAL COURTS

There is a hierarchy of several levels to the federal court system, each with a distinctive type of court: **district trial courts; circuit courts of appeal;** and the **United States Supreme Court.** Off to the side, in the shade of this federal judicial tree, are smaller courts of **Customs, Claims** and **Patent Appeals.** The vast majority of cases flow through the district and appeals courts; few find their way to the docket of the Supreme Court.

Federal District Courts are the busiest in the federal system. There are 94, one to four in every state and one each in Puerto Rico, Guam, the Virgin Islands and the Canal Zone. Each district court has a U. S. Attorney, U. S. Marshall, U. S. Magistrate, bankruptcy judge, probation officers, court clerk, and court reporter.

Federal Circuit Courts of Appeal function in eleven geographic sectors or jurisdictions called **circuits,** each with three to more than a dozen judges. These courts review decisions of federal district, tax, administrative, and state courts. They review all cases referred to them, as long as they are submitted according to proper procedure. As we will see, state appeals courts "pick and choose" and deny hearing many of the cases submitted to them.

United States Supreme Court is often described as "the highest court in the land." There are nine justices and they are appointed by the president with the approval of the U. S. Senate. This court reviews cases referred by appelants who are dissatisfied with decisions of lower state or federal courts of appeals. Of literally thousands of cases referred, less than 200 are accepted, based on their involvement in what the Court considers important constitutional or judicial issues and concerns.

STATE COURTS

State courts parallel the function of the federal court system. There are state trial, appelate and supreme courts. Their jurisdiction, rules and procedures are set by statute which means by written acts of the state legislature. Unlike the federal appeals courts, **state appelate courts** exercise much greater selectivity like the **U. S. Supreme Court,** most of them screening out more cases than they accept.

WHICH COURT?

While federal courts specialize in cases and questions of constitutional law and federal laws, rules and regulations enacted by U. S. Congress, they can and do get involved in state court decisions. This occurs when a **U. S. Court of Appeals** or the **U. S. Supreme Court** reviews cases first tried in state courts. It is also true that in some situations cases can be heard in state or federal court. Litigants choose the court they feel will be most receptive to their claim. This dual system arose because of the ambiguity of **Act III, Section 2** of the **U. S. Constitution** which does not clearly differentiate federal from state jurisdiction:

> The judicial power shall extend to all cases, in law and equity, arising under this Constitution, the laws of the United States and . . . controversies between two or more states; between a state and citizens of another state; between citizens of different states; between citizens of the same state claiming lands under grants of different states, and between a state, or the citizens thereof, and foreign states, citizens or subjects.

TYPES OF LAW

Legal scholars divide law into two types: **substantive** and **procedural. Substantive laws** are involved in substantive due process define what's legal. Rights and responsibilities are expressed in **civil statutes** which are rooted in the **Constitution's** commitment to human rights. Societal norms and the penalties for violating them (what is a crime) are expressed in **criminal statutes. Procedural laws,** also referred to as **adjective law** or **Rules of Civil Procedure,** are the "how to" rules and procedures by which substantive law is administered, enforced and revised. These are rooted in the common law commitment to fairness (**due process**). Like the state v. federal jurisdiction overlap, the boundaries between substantive and procedural law are not clearly delineated.

Constitutional law is local, state and federal law which describes fundamental guiding principles of government and of law, their relationship to the individual citizen, and how they are to be administered, interpreted, integrated, limited in application and how legislatively amended.

Statutory law is the body of written laws in state codes and state and federal legislative acts which define requirements, describe consequences for violation and the grounds for litigation and prosecution.

Case law, also referred to as **court law** or **judge's law,** is the body of data consisting of previous cases, or what has happened in similar cases in the past applied to present cases (**legal precedents).**

Common law is law based on custom, usage and tradition and often referred to as "the law of immemorial antiquity." It consists largely of legal precedents from "old" England and its origins in feudal times and the United States excluding statutory law.

Administrative law is the body of law established by local, state and federal agencies and is composed of rules, regulations, orders and decisions such as for radio and TV licensing (Federal Communications Commission), advertising and deceptive practices (Federal Trade Commission), income tax reporting and evasion (Internal Revenue Service), aircraft and pilot licensing, flight rules and air traffic control (Federal Aviation Administration), and tariffs (Interstate Commerce Commission), and the number of life boats on ocean liners like the Titanic (British Board of Trade).

Mental health law is the body of law which provides for due process procedures for temporary detention, civil or involuntary commitment in a mental hospital, the determination of competence to stand trial and the insanity defense. Definitions, grounds and procedures for these determinations vary from state to state and state to federal jurisdiction, but involuntary commitment to a mental institution usually requires legal proof to satisfy the "trier of fact" (**judge**) that the person to be committed is **dangerous to self or others** and **psychotic or suffering from a severe mental disorder** and therefore **in need of care** in an inpatient treatment facility (i.e. cannot independently meet the demands or needs of everyday living).

Civil law is based on local laws and legal procedures to settle disputes, resolve conflict, and protect and enforce the rights of citizens by making the **plaintiff** (complainant, the injured party) **whole** again. It is remedial, seeking **injunctive relief** to stop some actual or potentially dangerous action or situation or **monetary settlement** or **award** to **compensate** for damages.

Criminal law is punitive, to punish those who violate law by crimes of omission or commission. A **felony** is the most serious crime, punishable by death (**capital crime**) or imprisonment such as murder, rape, armed robbery, assault with a deadly weapon, arson, kidnapping, drug dealing, treason, or grand theft. A **misdemeanor** is of lesser seriousness, punishable by fine or local jail or prison farms as opposed to longer penitentiary sentences as for a felony. Typical misdemeanors are traffic tickets, possession of minimal amounts of illegal drugs (**controlled substances**), driving, hunting or fishing without a license, etc. To be convicted for a criminal offense, two legal concepts must be proven: that the defendant was aware the act was illegal (**actus rea**) and deliberately did it anyway (**mens rea**). The defendant must also be **legally competent**, that is, s/he must understand the charges, court procedure and communicate and cooperate with an attorney to assist in her or his defense.

TYPES OF TRIALS

There are two major types of trials in which expert witnesses testify: **civil** and **criminal.** Most states have adapted the **Federal Rules of Civil Procedure** for civil suits and the **Federal Rules of Criminal Procedure** for criminal cases. Civil pleadings (or proceedings) consist of filing a **complaint** by the party wronged (**plaintiff**), an **answer** admitting or denying the complaint by the party charged with wrongdoing (**defendant**), and a **reply** or response to the answer by the plaintiff. Civil proceedings can also involve motions to further clarify the issues such as for summary judgment, bill of particulars, to dismiss the case, judge the pleadings, or for more detailed information.

Criminal rules are quite similar to the civil rules and avoid many of the time-consuming complexities of common law. Judge Medina characterized the old common law practices as providing "members of the bench and bar with a source of continual intellectual amusement and pleasure, the sporting theory of justice. To win a lawsuit by guile and surprise or by the skillful manipulation of mysterious rules, understood only by the elite, was quite the thing to do." He concluded that applying **Federal Rules of Civil Procedure** "represents one of the twentieth century contributions to the improvement of judicial administration and the furtherance of effective, timely justice" (**Clark v. Pennsylvania Railroad, U. S. Ct. Appl., 1964 328 F.2d 591**).

A crime is alleged by **indictment** or **complaint** to which the defendant pleads **guilty, not guilty** or if allowed by the court, **nolo contendere.** Nolo contendere may suggest the name of a card shark at Vegas or perhaps a gourmet Italian restaurant, but it's really Latin for "I won't contest it." In criminal cases it is legally equivalent to a guilty plea but prevents civil action against the defendant for the same acts. It is used mostly in proven antitrust price-fixing cases where civil suits are very likely to follow. There can be motions in criminal cases for **bills of particulars,** or to **dismiss** or for **acquittal**.

TYPICAL CIVIL PROCEEDING

In most cases, a person (or **party**) who feels s/he has been wronged (**plaintiff**) consults an attorney who gathers data, reviews the facts, may or may not interview witnesses, then researches applicable laws and previous similar cases (**legal precedents**) and determine whether the case is **actionable.** If it is actionable and the plaintiff wants to proceed, a **complaint** or **petition** is formally filed in the appropriate court. It states the basis of the claim and the relief sought (**damages** or **judgment**). A **praecipe** (request) **for summons** is also filed requesting the court clerk to have a summons **served** on the **defendant** (the person charged with wrongdoing). This is the defendant's formal notification of suit.

The defendant can respond in any of several ways such as motions **to dismiss** (attempt to drop the case as not actionable), **to strike** (remove matter that is erroneous, improper, irrelevant or prejudicial), **to quash service of summons** (charging the summons was issued improperly) or **make more definite and certain** (request more detailed information). The defendant's formal written response to the plaintiff's complaint is known as **the answer.** It can contain a counterclaim for damages or relief and this is known as a **cross-complaint** or **cross-petition.** The plaintiff's response to the defendant is termed a **reply.** If there is an exchange of claims and answers, both defendant and plaintiff can issue replies.

There can be **interrogatories,** lists of written questions to defendants, plaintiffs or witnesses on either or both sides, and **depositions,** out-of-court sworn statements for use in court or to prepare for court. Testimony at depositions can involve cross-examination by the opposing attorney. They are not a public record unless a court order makes them so. These are further defined in Chapter 5.

There is a **pretrial hearing** attended only by attorneys on both sides and the judge. Here, both sides agree on undisputed facts (called **stipulations**) and agreed **points of law** or **matters at issue** to be decided in the case. This hearing sharpens the focus of the case and saves much court time. In many cases there is an out-of-court settlement because the basis of conflict is more clearly seen, contending facts known, and a solution more apparent. A section in Chapter 3, "As it happens" describes the trial process.

TYPICAL CRIMINAL PROCEEDING

Criminal charges against a defendant can be in the form of a **grand jury indictment** or a prosecuting attorney's **information.** Both are formal actions and they state the charge, date, time and place of the alleged crime. A **grand jury** is a state or federal select group usually of sixteen citizens with the sworn duty to investigate cases referred by the prosecuting attorney and decide whether or not a crime has been committed. Their deliberations are closed to the public. In some states, grand juries meet on a fixed schedule, but there can be **special grand juries** assigned to consider special situations. If there is an indictment or prosecutor's information, the court clerk will issue an **arrest warrant** for the police to apprehend the defendant. For major crimes (**felonies**), the defendant is first brought before a state magistrate or a U. S. Commissioner in federal cases. If **bail bond** is not posted or paid or the offense is not bailable, the defendant remains in custody until the case is resolved. In most jurisdictions, police can detain or hold a person in custody without formal charges for 24 hours pending investigation, but access to an attorney must be provided. If the individual can't afford to pay an attorney, legal services must be provided free of charge.

Except for grand jury indictments, a defendant can request a timely **preliminary hearing** before a magistrate where the prosecuting attorney must establish there is sufficient evidence that a crime has been committed. If there is, the defendant is **bound over** (referred) for trial and either released on bail or without it **on his own recognizance** (implied promise to appear for trial) or **remanded** into custody (returned to jail) until trial. If there is insufficient evidence to proceed to trial, charges are dismissed and the defendant "walks"—goes free. At a set date and time, the defendant is **arraigned:** charges are read, rights are explained, and the defendant is asked: "How do you plead?" A guilty plea to a misdemeanor usually results in immediate (and light) sentencing, although in some states arraignment and sentencing must be done at separate hearings. Pleading guilty to a felony results in scheduling a subsequent **sentencing hearing.**

Plea bargaining is negotiating and adjusting charges and consequent punishments. In some cases, defendants who cooperate by providing information which helps prosecute others of more serious crimes can be rewarded by reduced sentences or charges of lesser severity. Criminal charges can be eliminated altogether "by plea negotiations in which a defendant enters a plea of guilty or nolo contendere in the expectation that other charges will be dismissed or that sentence concessions will be granted" (American Bar Association, 1980).

Chapter 3 provides more details of trial procedures, and Chapters 5 and 6 more fully explain the role, function and practical realities of expert witness testimony. If time is short, you may find it helpful to read those chapters next. Chapter 2 and the Glossary at the back of this book are intended to provide you with background information for a better understanding of "the world of law." They are recommended especially for "browsing" while waiting to testify or for "curled-up shoes-off" casual perusal.

REFERENCES

American Bar Association (1983). For hire: Expert witness boom time. *American Bar Association Journal*, 69, 429.

American Bar Association (1980). *Law and the courts*. Chicago, IL: Author.

Black, H. C. (Ed.) (1979). *Black's law dictionary.* St. Paul, MN: West Publishing.

Hess, A. K. (1985). The psychologist as expert witness: A guide to the courtroom arena. *The Clinical Psychologist*, Fall 1985, p. 75.

Kester, J. G. (1987). Too many lawyers? *Reader's Digest,* April, 1987, 153-160.
Kurke, M. I., and Meyer, R. G. (Eds.) (1986). *Psychology in product liability and personal injury litigation.* Washington, DC: Hemisphere Publishing.
Morgan, N. E. (1987). The current litigation crisis and tort reform. *Journal of Medical Records Association,* January, 1987, 19-22.
Ostroff, P. I. (1982). Experts: A few fundamentals. *Litigation,* 8, 8-9 and 64.
Webb, K. B. (Ed.) (1951). *A source book of opinion on human values.* London, England: Tower Bridge.

CHAPTER 2

LAW AS IDEA AND IDEAL

Justice in the life
and conduct of the state
is possible only as it resides
in the hearts and souls of citizens.

Inscription,
Department of Justice
Washington, D. C.

LAW IS a societally accepted system of resolving conflicts and it is also an abstract ideal based on the natural moral order believed to permeate the universe. This has been a common element shared by all civilizations worldwide throughout history. It seems likely these ideas developed from the observed order and predictability of natural phenomena. Day always follows night, season regularly follows season, the sun rises and the moon phases and the same major stars reappear in the night sky. Perhaps the ancients sought to understand their own nature, human relationships and responsibilities in the orderly sequence of days and seasons on earth, and the precision of stars and planets in the heavens.

Cultural anthropologists and archaeologists (the scientists who study comparative cultures, their objects and artifacts) define law as "culturally established standards of behavior and guides to social interaction" which "creates a corresponding set of obligations" to conform to law by preserving peace and order and "contribute to the well-being of society" (Aceves and King, 1978, p. 186).

As societies evolved from the most primitive to the more sophisticated, the concepts of justice and law developed and along with these a growing need for a functioning legal process. Anthropologists trace this development from primitive often superstitious rites, with vaguely defined values and customs unique to the culture, to a multitude of written statutes and extensive libraries of case transcripts applied to formal, structured courtroom procedures. The theologian Saint Thomas Aquinas (351-430 A.D.) taught that law is given directly by God. It was logical, then, that the church should be the repository of law, and for centuries this was so. The British philosopher John Locke (1632-1704) changed the focus from church to man, from religion to philosophy and law of and by itself. He held that we discover reasonable rules of conduct from a God-given innate ability to differentiate right from wrong.

Thomas Jefferson (1743-1828) reflected this ideal with his characteristic simple elegance in the **Declaration of Independence** in 1776 which refers to "the laws of nature and nature's God." Mortimer Adler, editor of the **Great Books of the Western World** series, wrote that "the first precept of natural law is to seek the good and avoid evil" (1972). **The Golden Rule,** to do unto others what we would have done to us, follows from this precept and is the heart of common law, that great reservoir of legal philosophy and doctrine flowing across centuries of Old English and American history.

It is not at all surprising, then, that judges and lawyers hold such deep reverence for the idea and the ideal of law and justice. For most of them, law is as much a mission as a career. They believe that they themselves, by their knowledge, training, skill and experience can make a difference, in the case being argued, to the citizens involved directly and indirectly in it, now and in the future, to society itself. Law is for them a noble calling with deep conviction much like religious faith. Most of them are emotionally involved in it, much like a romance that never wanes, a passion that does not fade. It is an obsession that persists and reinforces itself every day in court, in the most hotly contested cases, amid the most frustrating even cynical feelings. It can be a love-hate relationship for them, but the reverence for law of and by itself remains long after irritation, disappointment and disillusionment have cooled. It has been so throughout history and law is an ancient profession. Few others have such deep historical roots. Anyone participating in the legal process should be aware of this great heritage.

Law, A Hallowed Tradition

Archaeological research documents an established legal system of courts and trial procedures in the most ancient civilizations. One of the most ancient judicial processes was the **Code of Hammurabi** established by the Babylonian King Hammurabi (1792-1750 B.C.). It was a rigid punitive system of retribution for wrongdoing. More than 300 of the statutes have been unearthed and preserved in museums throughout the world. Kramer (1956) has described the **Ur-Nammu tablets** from ancient Sumer, conservatively dated to 2050 B.C. If the dating is correct, these are the world's oldest records of a legal system. The tablets describe trial by jury. Monetary fines are substituted for punishment or dismemberment, humane treatment previously thought to have developed thousands of years later. The ancient Sumerians were using sophisticated legal procedures a thousand years before the **Old Testament** and Homer's **Iliad** and **Odyssey:**

> Law and justice were key concepts in ancient Sumer, in both theory and practice and Sumerian social and economic life was permeated by them. In the past century archaeologists have uncovered thousands of clay tablets inscribed with all sorts of Sumerian legal documents—contracts, deeds, wills, promissory notes, receipts, and court decisions. In ancient Sumer, the advanced student devoted much of his school time to the field of law and he constantly practiced the writing of the highly specialized legal terminology as well as of law codes and those court decisions which had taken on the force of legal precedents (Kramer, 1956, p. 51).

In ancient India, China and Arabia, the legal system reflected **the law of karma,** of cosmic destiny, consequences in future lives for conduct in the present. Still believed today by millions, it is the eternal law of cause and effect, that there is a punishment for every wrongdoing, without exception, if not in this life, then surely in the next in one of many rebirths. Reincarnation, the ongoing transmigration of souls through many existences, is an opportunity to educate and enlighten the soul in the path of light. Buddha broke the chain of endless rebirths and taught that one who leads a good life can achieve **nirvana** or perfect enlightenment and never return to an earthly existence.

History suggests that where religion and government are the same (a **theocracy**) there is a tendency toward strict social conformity and excessively rigid and punitive application of law (e.g. Spanish Inquisition, Salem and European witch trials). This was a major factor contributing to the emigration of the Puritans from Europe to America and the subsequent colonization elsewhere in "the New World." It led to the Constitutional doctrine of separation of church and state. William Ralph Inge (1860-1954), Professor of Divinity at Cambridge (1907-1911) and Dean of St. Paul's, London (1911-1934) observed that "the Church never goes into politics without coming out badly smirched" (Webb, 1951, p. 161).

Chamberlin and Feldman (1961) suspect ancient Babylonian and Egyption influences in the Old Testament **Book of Psalms** (c. 600-200 B.C., conjectured), not only a source for moral teachings but also a commentary on justice, law and order. The Jews used it widely as the Pentateuch and the Christians as the **Psalter.** Saint Augustine (354-430 A.D.) described it as "the language of devotion" and Martin Luther (1483-1546) considered it "the Bible in miniature." **Psalm 19** is of special interest, describing the interaction of God or the Creator and the natural, moral order of life:

God's Handiwork and God's Statutes

The heavens declare the glory of God
  and the firmament showeth his handiwork.
Day unto day uttereth speech,
  and night unto night showeth knowledge.
There is no speech or language
  where their voice is not heard.
Their line is gone out through all the earth.
  and their words to the end of the world . . .
The law of the Lord is perfect,
  restoring the soul.
The testimony of the Lord is sure,
  making wise of the simple.
The statues of the Lord are right,
  rejoicing the heart.
The commandment of the Lord is pure,
  enlightening the eyes.
The fear of the Lord is clean,
  enduring forever.
The judgments of the Lord are true
  and righteous altogether.
More to be desired than gold,
  yea, than much fine gold;
  sweeter also than honey and the honeycomb.
Moreover, by them is thy servant warned
  and in keeping them there is great reward.

The Hebrews distinguished themselves by their reverence for law, order and justice. The **Old Testament** contains many references and reaffirmations to these ideals. Two examples are the **Ten Commandments** of Moses (c. 1200 B.C.) and the legendary wisdom of King Solomon (c. 973-933 B.C.). Moses is sometimes referred to as "the lawgiver" and the commandments represent a formulation of a code of conduct, of values and morals. The fifth commandment is directly related to the legal process and the traditional courtroom rule forbidding perjury: "Thou shalt not bear false witness against they neighbor" (**Exodus,** 20:16). Though disputed by some biblical scholars, King Solomon is said to have authored several books of the **Old Testament**, most notably **Proverbs, Ecclesiasticus, Song of Solomon** and **Wisdom of Solomon.** Commins and Linscott (1947) contend the Psalms reflect more of a Greek influence, and the ancient Greeks had an impressive record of achievements.

Socrates, Plato, Aristotle and Sophocles are but a few of many exemplars of the aspirations and ideals of ancient Greece. Socrates (469-399 B.C.), Plato's teacher and mentor, had an established reputation for questioning community values which made him many enemies. Charged, tried and convicted of "corrupting youth" with his ideas, he was sentenced to death by poison (hemlock). Gracious to the end, Socrates's final words were taken down by Plato and passed down to us in **The Apology of Socrates:**

> Wherefore, O Judges, be of good cheer about death and know this of a truth, that no evil can happen to a good man either in life or after death. He and his approaching end happened by mere chance . . . for which reason I am not angry with my accusers or my condemners; they have done me no harm, although neither of them meant to do me any good, and for this I gently blame them.
>
> Still, I have a favor to ask of them. When my sons are grown up I would ask you, my friends, to punish them and I would have you trouble them as I have troubled you if they seem to care about riches or anything more than about virtue, or if they pretend to be something when they are really nothing. Then reprove them as I have reproved you, for not caring about that for which they ought to care, and thinking they are something when they are really nothing. And if you do this, I and my sons will have received justice at your hands.
>
> The hour of departure has arrived and we go our ways, I to die and you to live. Which is better only God knows (Eliot, 1909a, pp. 28-19).

Plato (427-347 B.C.) was twenty years old when he began his studies under Socrates. After Socrates's death, he travelled through Egypt and Italy, returning to Athens to found **The Academy,** a private institution which taught a free and open search for truth. Aristotle was a student there. Plato avoided the reactionary "gadfly" questioning of his mentor, Socrates, and he was often consulted by political leaders. In his 40 years directing **The Academy,** Plato wrote two works specific to law: **The Republic,** describing justice in the ideal state, and **Laws,** an unfinished work on the qualities of good law.

Plato contributed much to law theory. **Idea** and **the ideal form** are two powerful and meaningful concepts relevant to law and justice. The noblest ideal, the highest virtue, Plato taught, was harmony between the soul and the universe. This, incidentally, is also the basic tenet of **yoga** which really means yoking the spirit to the universe. This harmony Plato described in terms of **ideas** and it is achieved as reason controls behavior in a reflective, considerate, thoughtful state of mind. The legal doctrine of "reasonable" or "prudent" person is directly related to this Platonic concept. The greatest idea, Plato maintained, was God and the ideas of beauty and elegance follow and flow from it. He felt that the ideal state would be ruled by a philosopher-king who epitomized these pure ideals in his own life, leadership and thought.

Aristotle (384-322 A.D.) as has been noted was Plato's student. He left **The Academy** to be tutor to Alexander the Great. He later returned to Athens and founded his own school which taught ethics, logic, science, metaphysics, politics, poetics and rhetoric. The light of Socrates was continued in the life and work of Plato and Aristotle, a rich legacy unparalleled in history. Indeed, if the Athenian court which convicted Socrates had the benefit of expert witness testimony of his students, his life may have been spared. Certainly, the jury did not follow Plato's idea and ideals concepts. "The law," Aristotle wrote, "is reason free of passion" and "the law is order; good law is good order" (**Politics,** Chap. 4). "Even when laws have been written down," he observed, "they ought not always to remain unaltered" (ibid., Chap. 8).

Sophocles (c. 496-406 B.C.) was a contemporary of Socrates who wrote more than 100 plays and was awarded many honors and prizes for his playwriting. He is credited with mastering the **morality play,** a powerful device demonstrating natural moral law and drawing the audience into shared emotions through the **Greek chorus** which as a voice of conscience chanted warnings to the players on stage. His tragedy, **Oedipus Rex,** inspired Sigmund Freud to formulate the theory of the Oedipus complex and the unconscious mind. Another tragedy, **Antigone,** had similar impact on the development of law as a reflection of higher ideals and the natural moral law. It is also a touching story of love and selfless duty. Many legal scholars consider **Antigone** to be a major contribution to the development of common law.

Antigone's brother Polynices participated in an unsuccessful attack against the city-state after his brother Eteocles banished him. Eteocles did so to eliminate his brother as a successor to King Creon, their uncle. Both Polynices and Eteocles were killed in the battle. King Creon decreed under penalty of death that Eteocles would get an honorable burial as defender of the city-state, but Polynices, a traitor, would be left where he fell, food for birds of prey. The Greek chorus chants the king's justification: "When laws are kept, how proudly the city stands! When laws are broken, what of the city then?" (Grant, 1962). Antigone loved both her brothers and she announces her intention to bury Polynices.

King Creon calls Antigone before him and tells her that to bury Polynices is to commit treason. She replies that even though she violates his law she must obey a **higher law,** love for her brother, for family, for love itself, pure and good. Creon informs her that all laws change and we can only follow the law of the day which is his law. She does not relent: "The unwritten laws of God know not change. They are not of today nor yesterday but live forever, nor can man assign when first they sprang into being" (Grant, 1962, p. 257). Like Pilate, like Socrates's jurors, Creon decrees the death penalty. She is to be buried alive.

A blind prophet warns Creon that the gods are angry at this "double sin of detaining the dead with the living and the living with the dead." Creon is unmoved. The blind man prophesies the king's son will die as vengeance of the gods. Creon reflects on this and pardons Antigone. Happy ending? Not in ancient Greece! Before she is notified, Antigone kills herself. The king's son, in love with her, kills himself in despair. Creon's wife, hearing of these events, also kills herself, cursing Creon for causing their son's death.

Plutarch (46-129 A.D.) was a Greek biographer who taught in Rome and was a master at character studies of Greeks and Romans from earliest times to his own. One of the historical personalities he described was Solon (c. 638-559 B.C.), an "Athenian lawgiver" who was "son of the Seven Wise Men of Greece." Plutarch reported that Solon was elected Archon by his fellow citizens and given full power to initiate reform. He reorganized the Senate and the lower house. He repealed laws he considered too severe such as "those that stole a cabbage or an apple to suffer even as villains that committed sacrilege or murder" (Plutarch, 1947). To serve on a jury "first seemed nothing but afterwards was found an enormous privilege, as almost every matter of dispute came before them." He established appeals courts, wills and personal-injury lawsuits.

In the Roman Empire there were similar voices. Marcus Aurelius (125-180 A.D.) was emperor from 161 A.D. until his death in 180 A.D. He was a professed opponent of Christianity because he saw it as an attempt to place religion above the state. To him, God was within human nature and the state, composed of people, reflected divine law. He believed there is a basic duty to obey the divine law of reason which is within everyone. When a society does this, peace and harmony result:

> You can pass life happily if you go the right way and if you can think and act the right way. These two are common to the soul of God and man.
>
> So retire into yourself. The rational principle that rules the universe has this nature. It is content with itself when it does what is just and in so doing achieves serenity (**Meditations**).

Marcus Aurelius conceived the universe as a divine and human interaction or interplay of these two basic factors. In **Meditations** he wrote that there is "one universe made up of all that is and one God in it all and one principle of being and one law, reason, shared by all thinking creatures" (**Chap. 7**).

Cicero (106-43 B.C.) wrestled with the realities of applying divine law to human foibles a century before Marcus Aurelius. Eliot (1909c) described Cicero as "the greatest of Roman orators" and his distinguished accomplishments warrant the title. He was throughout his career a persuasive speaker of great skill and eloquence. More than fifty of his speeches are still available to us. They are sharply honed, well reasoned, focussing sharply on the details of the case being argued and an excellent example of effective trial technique.

Cicero achieved greatness in a variety of appointive and elective offices in the legal and judicial systems of ancient Rome. He led impeachment proceedings of a governor for "corruption in office." He exposed and overthrew a conspiracy of patricians led by Cataline. His luck changed for the worse when he supported Pompey against Julius Caesar in 48 B.C. In 44 B.C. he made a strategic error by opposing Mark Anthony after Caesar's assassination. A year later he was killed by followers of Mark Anthony.

MODERN EUROPEAN HISTORY

Characteristic of world history, strong cultures and traditions compete—and merge. The ideas and ideals of the Hebrews, Greeks, Romans and Christians slowly fused together awaiting the next great awakening. For law and justice, that time was 1215 A.D., at Runnymede, England. King John was forced by the barons to sign the **Magna Carta.** The purpose was to establish the autonomy of the barons, towns and churches, but it also protected the rights and freedom of individual citizens. But in those days kings believed they themselves had "the divine right of kings" and safely out of danger, John renounced his signature. The Pope declared him not subject to it (this was long before Henry VIII and the establishment of the Church of England). The result was civil war. John lost. This time he signed a revised document called **The Charter of Liberties** or **The Great Charter.** It ended forever the doctrine of the divine right of kings and made the law equally binding to all—even kings. An excerpt from the original **Magna Carta**:

> No freeman shall be taken, or imprisoned, or outlawed, or exiled, or in any way harmed, nor will we go upon him nor will we send upon him, except by the legal judgment of his peers or by the law of the land (**Clause 39**).

The **Renaissance** began in Italy in the fourteenth century and spread throughout Europe inspiring the **Age of Enlightenment** which followed. During these centuries there was a reawakening of interest in the historical and cultural roots of the Western political heritage. The **Protestant Reformation** fanned the fires of change and political revolutions erupted in the American colonies and France. The printing press made the **Bible** and other literature accessible to many more readers. Eloquent spokesmen gave voice to the ferment and the feelings, the issues and concerns, hopes, needs and values.

William Shakespeare (1564-1616) wove into his plays higher truths intertwined with the crude realities of everyday life in the tradition of Sophocles's morality plays. In **Henry VI** he wrote: "In thy face I see the map of honor, truth and loyalty . . . what stronger breastplate than a heart untainted? Thrice is he armed that has his quarrel just." Thomas Hobbes (1588-1679) reaffirmed the basic tenets of natural, moral law in his **Leviathan** written in 1651: "The laws of nature, as justice, equity, modesty, mercy and in sum doing to others as we would be done to." John Milton (1608-1674) wrote in his **Doctrine and Discipline of Divorce** (1643) that "truth is impossible to be soiled by any outward touch just as the sunbeam."

John Locke (1632-1704) described free, enlightened citizens as being in "a state of nature," of dignity, integrity and purity. This concept inspired the American colonists who were growing increasingly frustrated with British rule and what they considered the capricious attitude of King George III. In his **Two Treatises on Civil Government** Locke wrote: "Nature has a law . . . which obliges everyone and reason which is that law" that "no one ought to harm another in his life, health, liberty or possessions" (Commins & Linscott, 1947, p. 60). "Men are naturally free . . . and governments begun in peace had their beginning laid on that foundation and were made by the consent of the people" (ibid., p. 116).

To form an ideal society, Locke claimed that people "give up the equality, liberty and executive power they had in the state of nature" for "the good of society . . . to preserve self, liberty and property." The power of society cannot then violate the common good because those in power are "bound to govern by established standing laws promulgated and known to the people, not by extemporary decrees" but by "indifferent and upright judges . . . to no other end but the peace, safety and public good of the people" (ibid., p. 132).

Jonathan Swift (1667-1745) was a contemporary of John Locke and an influential political satirist. His most famous work was **Gulliver's Travels** (1726) which was a parody of politics, law, courts and statesmanship. Despite his cynicism, though, there is a reverence for ideals. For example, Gulliver describes how the Lilliputian courts dispense rewards as well as punishments. Their statue of justice, Swift described as "formed with six eyes, two before, as many behind, and on each side one, to signify circumspection; with a bag of gold open in her right hand and a sword sheathed in her left, to show she is more disposed to reward than to punish" (Swift, 1947, p. 367). If citizens "observed the laws . . . for seventy-three moons" they received "certain privileges . . . with a proportionate sum of money out of a fund appropriated for that use" (ibid., p. 366).

Immanuel Kant (1724-1804) concluded his **Critique of Pure Reason** (1781) with the observation that "two things fill the mind with ever-increasing wonder and awe, the more often and the more intensely the mind of thought is drawn to them: the starry heavens above me and the moral law within me." His conviction is quite similar to that in **Psalm 19** ("The heavens declare the glory of God . . . their line is gone out through all the earth"). But Kant reverses the process, suggesting we consider the result or effect of our actions as if they would become absolute: "There is only a single categorical imperative and it is this: act only on that maxim through which you can at the same time will that it should become a universal law" (**The Metaphysics of Morals,** 1797, Chapter 11).

Kant, like those we have previously sampled, confirms the divine-human interaction of God/Creator and humanity: "The moral law reveals to me a life independent of animality and even of the whole sensible world, at least so far as may be inferred from the determination assigned to my existence by this law, a destination not restricted to conditions and limits of this life but reaching into the infinite" (**Critique of Practical Reason**).

John Dryden (1631-1700) added to the growing belief in truth as self-evident in his **The Hind and the Panther** (1687): "Truth has such a face and such a mien as to be loved needs only to be seen" (I, line 32). A generation later, Voltaire (1694-1778) echoed Dryden's perception: "It is the modest, not the presumptuous, inquirer who makes a real and safe progress in the discovery of divine truths. One follows Nature and Nature's God; that is, follows God in his works and in his word" (letter to Cardinal de Bernis, 1761). In a speech in 1794, Edmund Burke (1729-1797) said: "There is but one law for all, namely that law which governs all law, the law of our Creator, the law of humanity, justice, equity, the law of nature and of nations."

EARLY AMERICAN HISTORY

Jean Jacques Rousseau (1712-1778) was an impulsive, restless Swiss-born political activist. Due to his antagonistic manner, controversy followed him all his life. In Paris he published **The Social Contract** (1762), a work whose influence crossed the Atlantic and added to the revolutionary ferment in the American colonies. He maintained that government is in fact a social contract between "natural men" uncorrupted by the world, a "political body (which) is a real contract between the people and the chiefs chosen by them; a contract by which both parties bind themselves to observe the laws therein expressed which form the ties of their union" (Commins and Linscott, 1947, p. 283).

The "terms" of Rousseau's "contract" are that citizens "concentrate all their will in one" and the resulting unified will is **law** "obligatory on all . . . without exception." It is the **Magna Carta** restated. But Rousseau took it a step further, expanding basic rights and freedom into a broader mandate of public well-being. "There is little inequality in nature," he wrote, and the inequality in society exists because of "our faculties and the advance of the human mind . . . property and laws." Rousseau claimed it is "plainly contrary to the law of nature . . . that children should command old men, fools wise men" or that "a privileged few should gorge themselves with superfluities when the starving multitude are in want of the bare necessities of life" (ibid., p. 293).

Even before the American Revolution, these ideas and ideals were being applied in the colonies. In 1770, none other than John Adams (1735-1826), later to succeed Washington as president, defended the British soldiers who participated in the Boston massacre. It was an early test of justice for the angry colonists. Here is a brief excerpt of Adams' defense:

> The law no passion can disturb. 'Tis void of desire and fear, lust and anger . . . The law in all vicissitudes of government, fluctuations of the passions, or flights of enthusiasm, will preserve a steady, undeviating course; it will not bend to the uncertain wishes, imaginations and wanton tempers of men . . . . 'Tis deaf, inexorable, inflexible. On the one hand it is inexorable to the cries and lamentations of the prisoners. On the other hand, it is deaf, deaf as an adder, to the clamors of the populace.

John Jay (1745-1829) was President of the Continental Congress (1778-1779) and later Chief Justice of the U. S. Supreme Court (1789-1795). He wrote that "justice is always the same whether it be from one man to a million or from a million to one man." Adams, Franklin and Jefferson, to name but a few, sought to make these and other ideals everyday realities in the new American republic. Four of the ten amendments to the **Constitution** which comprise the **Bill of Rights** deal with the courts and legal process. "The laws of nature and of nature's God" are specified in the **Declaration of Independence** as are self-evident truths and "certain unalienable rights." These words and principles echo far back in world history.

THEORY INTO PRACTICE

In the decades which followed the **Declaration of Independence** and the ratification of the **Constitution,** the challenge was to continue the work of the founding fathers and to maintain relevance with the principles they set forth. It was no simple task, because American society grew more complex and every court case introduced new and often confusing factors.

John Marshall (1755-1835) was a Chief Justice of the U. S. Supreme Court (1801-1835) and he resolved many basic questions and conflicts of constitutional law during his 35 years on the court. His philosophy of law is contained in his opinion in the **McCulloch vs. Maryland** case in 1819 in which he stated that the Constitution "would endure for ages to come and consequently would be adapted to the various crises of human offices." Henry Clay (1775-1852) was a Congressman, Speaker of the House of Representatives, U. S. Senator, Secretary of State and an unsuccessful presidential candidate in 1832 and again in 1844. He was a practical man and a skilled negotiator who gained the nicknames "The Great Compromiser" and "the Great Pacificator." Clay emphasized the value of precedent, of applying previous experience in similar situations: "precedents deliberately established by wise men are entitled to great weight." Henry Ward Beecher (1813-1887) was an outspoken, influential clergyman who championed women's rights and anti-slavery. He joined in the legion of legal and political philosophers described in this chapter and summed up its commitment and its ideal: "The philosophy of one century is the common sense of the next."

Intent and **precedent** are two very important features of the theory and practice of law. Laws are attempts to translate and then to apply divine, natural, moral law into the common sense practical resolution of material or worldly conflicts. In contested cases attorneys vigorously debate the "intent" of the law and the intent of defendants and plaintiffs. The court, the "trier of fact," decides whether or not the case presented satisfies statutory requirements and the legal criteria for proof. A common method of legal proof of intent is to research then report testimony, verdicts or awards from previous similar cases from the past (**precedent**).

Oliver Wendell Holmes (1841-1935) was Professor of Law at Harvard Law School (1882), Chief Justice of the Massachusetts Supreme Court (1899-1902) and Associate Justice on the U. S. Supreme Court (1902-1932). He was a renowned expert on justice and law, a prolific writer and an eloquent speaker. In 1911 he wrote **The Common Man** which described what law is and should be. Here is an excerpt from it:

> The life of the law has not been logic. It has been experience . . . the law embodies the story of a nation's development through many centuries and it cannot be dealt with as if it contained only the axioms and corollaries of a book of mathematics . . . to know what it is we must know what it has been and what it tends to become. We must alternately consult history and existing theories of legislation. But the most difficult labor will be to understand the combination of the two products into new products at every stage.

The history and development of law from idea to ideal, theory to practice, is a reflection of the world's search for truth and justice from earliest civilization to tomorrow's newspaper. At the founding of the United Nations in 1945, President Harry S. Truman commented that "justice is the greatest power on earth" and "to that tremendous power alone will we submit." In 1948, the United Nations adopted a **Universal Declaration of Human Rights** which read in part: "A fundamental right is the right of free movement in the search for truth and in the attainment of moral good and justice and also the right to a dignified life."

Law as idea and ideal is alive and well, a torch passed to each succeeding generation. It does not always burn brightly, but it has never been extinguished. Its language and its principles remain despite disappointing setbacks of wars and civil disorder, cruel human rights violations and international crime. Thomas Mann (1875-1955), Nobel laureate (1929), wrote in his **Idea of Justice** that "justice is the dominant idea of the epoch and its realization as far as is humanly possible has become a matter of world conscience from which there is no escape and which can no longer be neglected."

In 1939, during the troubled years prior to World War II, George Catlin wrote in **The Anglo-Saxon Tradition**:

> There is a grand tradition of human values, certain values constituting the very norms of civilization, agreed upon by men of insight throughout the centuries . . . Ideas are more real, more influential in operation, than individual men . . . . Our truth and tradition are not limited to ourselves . . . Native in its growth . . . potentially universal in its application . . .
>
> The notes of humanism are the appeal to reason, against mere brute dogma believed because the mass sentiment of some united society wills it to be believed; the raising of self-consciousness of the individual . . . and choice, including moral choice of community; preference for experiment and experience rather than for **a priori** metaphysical systems; attachment to learning and scholarship; belief in tradition from ancient times, expressing deeper truths of human nature which, although it might be broken by barbarism, may not have its value destroyed; and the attachment of importance to the judgment of the learned throughout the ages concerning what that tradition may be.

In 1913, one year before World War I, Justice Oliver Wendell Holmes wrote in **Law and the Court**: "We, too, need education in the obvious, to learn and transcend our own convictions and to leave room for much that we hold dear to be done away with, short of revolution, by the orderly change of law."

Political realities, the rise and fall of governments, two world wars that killed millions and many other lesser disputes as destructive to life and dreams, dimmed the torch of truth, law and justice. The words of Holmes, Catlin and Truman bridged three generations and three major wars joining with each other and with all those described in these pages. It is the same deep commitment shared by judges and attorneys everywhere. It is a personal, emotional involvement, a sacred love, a romance that never wanes. It is a loyalty to an ancient profession, daily renewed and reinforced. The inscription over the Pennsylvania Avenue entrance to the Department of Justice building in Washington sums it up well: "The place of justice is a hallowed place."

You, as an expert witness, have a very special privilege to participate in this process, this divine experiment which has been evolving thousands of years. It is as ancient as history itself, transcending language and culture, reflecting civilizations' highest ideals. As an expert witness you share in this sacred heritage and its noble purpose: to reach from self to nature to nature's God, to understand and apply truth to law and justice.

REFERENCES

Aceves, S. N., and King, H. G. (1978). *Cultural anthropology.* Morristown, NJ: Silver Burdett.

Adler, M. J. (1972). *Great ideas from the Great Books.* New York: Pocket Books.

Bartlett, J. (Ed.) (1968). *Familiar quotations: A collection of passages, phrases and proverbs traced to their sources in ancient and modern literature.* Boston: Little, Brown.

Catlin, G. (1939). *The Anglo-Saxon tradition.* London, England: Routledge and Kegan.

Chamberlin, R. B., and Feldman, H. (Eds.) (1961). *The Dartmouth Bible.* Second edition. Boston: Houghton-Mifflin.

Commins, S., and Linscott, R. N. (Eds.) (1947). *Man and the state: The political philosophers.* New York: Random House.

Ehrlich, L. (1947). The trial of John Brown. In A. Curiae (Ed.), *Law in action: An anthology of law in literature.* New York: Bonanza Books.

Eliot, C. W. (Ed.) (1909a). *The apology: Phaedo and Crito of Plato.* Jewett translation. Harvard Classics, Volume 2. New York: P. F. Collier.

Eliot, C. W. (Ed.) (1909b). *Nine Greek dramas.* Harvard Classics, Volume 8. New York: P. F. Collier.

Eliot, C. W. (Ed.) (1909c). *Letters of Marcus Tullius Cicero.* Harvard Classics, Volume 9. New York: P. F. Collier.

France, A. (1947). Crainquebille. In A. Curiae (Ed.), *Law in action: An anthology of law in literature.* New York: Bonanza Books.

Grant, M. (1962). *Myths of the Greeks and the Romans.* New York: World Publishing.

Kramer, S. N. (1956). *From the tablets of Sumer.* Indian Mills, CO: Falcon's Wing Press.

Plutarch (1947). The laws of Solon. In A. Curiae (Ed.), *Law in action: An anthology of law in literature.* New York: Bonanza Books.

Swift, J. (1947). The laws of the Lilliputians. In A. Curiae (Ed.), *Law in action: An anthology of law in literature.* New York: Bonanza Books.

Webb, K. B. (Ed.) (1951). *A source book of opinion on human values.* London, England: Tower Bridge.

CHAPTER 3

LAW: THE REALITIES

We have two codes of law:
One of honor and one of
the law courts
And they frequently collide.
—Michel de Montaigne
(1533-1592)
A Magistrate of Bordeaux

THOSE WITH little or no experience in court are likely to have an idealized notion of what happens there. The previous chapter reinforces such idealism, a perception of judges and attorneys joined together in a knightly quest for truth and justice. The statue of blind justice holding the scales symbolizes the ideal of due process, the sacred right of every citizen to be heard before an impartial court, the trier of fact, which feels for the balance, wielding the double-edged sword, cutting through opinion to truth. That's the ideal. Regrettably, it is not always realized.

Reality is that court is neither a peaceful, democratic process nor a mutually supportive, open sharing of fact and opinion. It is (intentionally) a conflict situation, a contest between two opposing sides, each represented by attorneys with sworn duties to do all they can to effectively represent their client and win the case. Webster's **Ninth New Collegiate Dictionary** (1983) defines "trial" as "the action or process of trying or putting to the proof; to test . . . " (p. 1258).

As we saw in Chapter 2, the legal process has evolved from diverse cultures over thousands of years of experimentation and experience. Though there are sometimes dramatic differences in legal procedures from one nation to another, all have a court system, a documented philosophy of justice, volumes of law codes, defining legal process and extensive files of trial transcripts. Regardless of language and cultural differences there is a common factor which joins them together: the so-called **adversary system**. Attorneys represent clients or state or federal governments in legal contests "nobody wants but nobody wants to lose." They confront each other in court as adversaries, advocates, champions for their particular cause.

To the lay public, courtroom procedure and the behavior of opposing attorneys in a hotly contested case may seem rude and unprincipled, even inappropriate or unethical. As difficult as it may be to accept, there is an underlying positive legal doctrine and ideal, that the truth is more likely to emerge between two antagonists who wage active verbal warfare rather than by a calm, dispassionate exchange of views. In most civil cases there were relatively passive, open exchanges of opinions which were unsuccessful before suit was filed.

In court, charges and countercharges, opposing facts and contradictions vividly contrast one side against the other so that the judge or jury can observe, understand and evaluate the difference, weigh merits of each side and better perceive the truth. As Ralph Waldo Emerson observed, "You can't thoroughly understand a truth until you have contended against it." That is the reality of the legal process.

COURT AS DRAMA

Court is a visually distinctive place, as much so as a library or church. Most courts even have a distinctive odor which to me is like a blend of a library and church or synagogue. Some courtrooms are traditional with wood panelling, wood furniture, high ceilings and oil paintings, usually portraits of judges or historical personalities long since deceased. Some courtrooms are modern, with abstract art or decor and indirect lighting much like a movie set for **Star Wars.** Regardless of furniture and decor there is a sameness about courtrooms everywhere, in this country and abroad. They are recognizable for what they are.

There is always an elevated platform up front where the judge sits so that judges are always "above" the proceedings, to "oversee" the process literally and figuratively. This is "the bench" and some are large, foreboding, far removed from the "stage." There is always a "jury box," a section set aside for up to twelve jurors usually off to the judge's side but lower and close to the "witness box" to better see and hear testimony. Plaintiff and defendant attorneys, the two adversaries or antagonists in the courtroom drama, have tables adjacent to each other facing the bench but at a discrete distance for some degree of privacy. Each has several chairs for attorney, client and co-counsel, if any. The court reporter sits near the judge, "on stage" to better hear testimony. Seats for the "audience," the family, friends, media and spectators, are placed theatre-like between the entrance doors and the court. There is usually a railing or low partition that separates the "audience" from the "cast." Bailiffs, uniformed court police, stand at or near the entrance doors to keep order, take custody of the defendant or jury, and to assist the court as needed.

Onto this stage step the cast, complete with costumes and props. The judge wears a black robe symbolizing the solemnity of the situation. It's interesting that judges dress the same, male or female. Most judges have papers arranged in front of them. I've caught them doodling as I testified (no reflection on the quality of my presentation, of course). Attorneys usually dress conservatively, men in business suits and women tastefully and professional. Loud, gaudy clothing and flashy jewelry are seldom if ever seen. They carry briefs (hence the name **briefcases**), sometimes books and papers, and they spread them out in front of them. Experienced attorneys vie for advantage by their voices and bodies (verbal and nonverbal behaviors) since costuming and casting (role and function) are not distinctive.

Uniformed bailiffs, with guns and badges, are visible reminders to all that the process will be orderly and without interruption or interference. The court drama begins with the bailiff, like a town crier of old, stating loudly something like: "All rise . . . " and continues, identifying the court, the judge (who enters and walks to his place), and the case title. In many courts, this announcement is delivered in a wailing monotone reminiscent of the Moslem call to prayer. Trial procedure is a script always the same with respect to casting and places on stage, sequence of events (who speaks first, next and last) and plot development (opening statements, testimony, cross-examination, closing statements, verdict).

While many movies take "editorial liberties" and exaggerate reality, there are some which provide an excellent orientation for those not familiar with courtroom procedures. With so many videotape recorders in use and local rental stores and clubs, the reader may find it helpful to view them—more than once if you feel especially insecure. The following are recommended:

Inherit the Wind (1960), a dramatization of the famous Scopes "monkey trial" in a traditional Tennessee courtroom. Spencer Tracy plays Clarence Darrow, Frederic March is William Jennings Bryan and Gene Kelly (without his dancing shoes!) plays the iconoclastic **Baltimore Sun** reporter H. L. Mencken. Some brilliant dialogue and performances enrich this legal and historic classic case.

Witness for the Prosecution (1957) is based on Agatha Christie's play and stars Charles Laughton as defense attorney, Marlene Dietrich as defendant and accused murderess, and Tyrone Power. This case illustrates rules of evidence and the difficulty in the use of circumstantial evidence when there are no eyewitnesses to the crime. Staged in a British court, it provides an opportunity to compare English with American procedures, more similar than dissimilar.

The Verdict (1982) is based on Barry Reed's novel and stars Paul Newman as a one-down defense attorney trying valiantly for a comeback and his protagonist James Mason, a polished, crafty senior partner in an established, prestigious law firm. It's a medical malpractice case and a good representation of courtroom strategies, rules of evidence, and how legal procedures can suppress some of the truth.

Jagged Edge is a suspense thriller based on a murder trial, and a large part of the film involves courtroom testimony. Jeff Bridges plays the role of a man accused of murdering his wife. The evidence is largely circumstantial. The plot is similar to **Witness for the Prosecution** but takes place in an American and not an English court and, unlike the British film, the accused is a man and the defense attorney is a woman.

AS IT HAPPENS

Court is drama and it has a script, cast, plot and a good deal of ritual. There is a chronology, an orderly, predictable sequence of events and this is divided into two phases: **pretrial** and **trial**. Pretrial procedures outline as follows:

PRETRIAL PHASE:

- Initial contact
- Expert or consultant?
- Pleadings
- Praecipe for summons
- Interrogatories?
- Depositions?
- Pretrial conference?

Initial Contact

Your involvement in the legal system as an expert witness or expert consultant begins when an attorney first contacts you by phone, mail or in person. Generally, phone calls are quicker and easier than letters and they are, as we will see in Chapter 5, less "discoverable" by the opposing attorney. A letter can be subpoenaed into evidence and you can be asked to describe a phone call in detail, but it can only be recalled and described verbally, some time after it took place.

You should, however, as routine practice note the date, time of call and its length, attorney's name and details of the conversation in the event you need it later. In my exerience, whenever I have been asked while testifying about phone calls from attorneys, they have been attempts to suggest bias transferred from attorney to myself. I was asked to describe what was discussed, questions asked, the number of calls made and by whom. I hardly ever phone attorneys, they phone infrequently, and the calls are short (less than 10 minutes). Many times I talk with the attorney's secretary or a paralegal assistant and thus avoid getting into details of the case. Keeping a record of calls as suggested will help you counter charges your opinion has been contaminated by the attorney requesting your testimony. Most attorneys are careful about what they say and write to you because it can be used in "courtroom combat." You, too, should be cautious in this regard.

Expert Consultant

You may be asked to serve as an expert witness or as an expert consultant. They are not the same. Expert consultants provide attorneys with specialized information, opinions, research or reports, which are **not** (supposed to be) **discoverable** by the opposing attorney. In cases where consultants are used, it's likely both sides will use them to complete informational needs for attorneys to fully understand their case, the strengths and weaknesses, and to plan the best strategy. As a general rule, expert consultants do not testify.

Expert Witness

Expert witnesses also provide specialized information, opinions, research or reports needed by an attorney, but they are expected to testify and the attorney asking for their help to identify them by name to the court (and so to the opposing attorney). Expert witnesses pretrial and trial statements are discoverable. You, as an identified witness, are also discoverable personally and professionally. If your testimony is important in the case, the opposing attorney will be very interested in investigating your background and credentials.

Pleadings

During the pretrial phase, **pleadings** are filed. These are a **complaint** or **petition** filed by the plaintiff describing the basis of litigation, damages claimed, ruling or other legal relief sought. The defendant files an **answer.** This back-and-forth action can continue, but in most cases one exchange of complaint and answer is sufficient.

Praecipe for Summons

This is a formal request to the court to issue a summons to the defendant which is the official legal notice of legal action.

Interrogatories? Depositions?

Interrogatories are not always involved in a case, so you will not always have to contend with them. They are written questions you respond to in writing. Depositions are pretrial hearings at which opposing attorneys interrogate you under oath and your responses are recorded. Usually, you're asked for additional details or to clarify your responses to the interrogatories. You should, of course, be consistent. There should be no difference in the content of interrogatories and depositons. If there are, you can be certain the opposing attorney will use discrepancies to disqualify or discredit your testimony. If you've been consistent, the opposing attorney is likely to lead you into making contradictory statements in cross-examination toward the same end.

Depositions and interrogatories are not available to the public or to the press, but defense and plaintiff or prosecuting attorneys and the judge have access to them. Attorneys **discover** what evidence will be presented from these pretrial documents. They explore each other's case material and can get a fairly good idea of what to expect later in court.

Pretrial Conference

After all this initial pretrial paperwork is processed, there is usually a **pretrial conference.** This is a closed session between the judge and both attorneys—clients (defendant or plaintiff) are not present. It is intended to provide discussion and agreement on the points of law in dispute, narrowing the focus to them and thus saving courtroom time and expense.

There is agreement also on certain undisputed facts and ground rules and these are called **stipulations.** Pretrial conferences provide a good review of legal merits of both sides and this often results in settlement of the case without the need to go to trial.

TRIAL PHASE

After the pretrial phase, if it is decided to proceed to trial, the following sequence takes place:

TRIAL PHASE:
- Subpoena
- Opening Statements
  - Plaintiff/prosecutor
  - Defendant
- Direct examination ← re-open direct examination
- Cross examination
- Redirect examination
- Recross examination → re-open direct examination
- Rebuttal
- Surrebuttal
- Closing arguments
- Verdict

Subpoena

As an expert witness, you will be served a subpoena issued by the court clerk and presented to you by a process server. It "commands you" to appear in court on a certain date and at a specified time. In some courts, usually in small towns, arrangements can be made for you to testify early, especially if you are a professional or sole proprietor of a business. The attorney requesting your testimony, or a member of his or her staff, could phone you when it is nearing time for your testimony. In these ways, you need not sit in the witness room waiting for hours.

It is not all that unusual for there to be a difference between the time typed on the subpoena and the actual time of testimony. This is due to delays during the trial process. Witnesses have waited all day and been asked to return the next. Most expert witnesses charge for their time while at court, testifying or waiting to testify. These are matters you will want to clarify at or soon after initial contact by the attorney requesting your testimony. It's also not unusual for expert witness testimony to be cancelled even after being subpoenaed.

Opening Statements

After the bailiff announces the trial proceeding ("All rise . . . ," etc.), the judge opens the trial by providing a summary of the legal basis involved and general statements of routine and any special conditions that may apply. The plaintiff's attorney then makes an **opening statement** describing that side of the case. The language usually includes "we will prove . . . " or "demonstrate that . . . " and at this stage no evidence or much detail are provided. The defense then makes its **opening statement,** using similar general language also devoid of details and specific evidence. Appleman (1967) contends that 65 percent of jurors form an opinion on the case at this early introductory stage.

Next, the **plaintiff's case** is presented, followed by the **defendant's case.** It is at this stage that witnesses are called, recalled, not called at all, or dismissed without testifying, depending on the course of combat taking place. Attorneys will at this stage use all the detail and evidence they feel important to their case.

Qualifying and Direct Examination

Subpoenaed, you report to the court clerk on the day and at the time specified. You will probably be **sequestered** in a room alone or with other witnesses. Sometimes attorneys agree to allow all the witnesses to sit in the courtroom during the proceedings. However, most attorneys don't want witnesses to hear all the details of the case, because it may affect or condition their opinion. Being a spectator at any event can involve you personally to some degree, be it a sports event, a movie or a courtroom drama.

I've been allowed to be in court with the other experts at the start of a criminal trial while the attorneys argued as to which witnesses could remain and which were to be sequestered. It reminded me of two kids choosing sides for a ball game in the neighborhood or younger kids playing "mine's better 'n yours." This mini-battle ended with all witnesses being locked away until needed. In another criminal case, I was sequestered six hours with expert witnesses testifying on the opposing side! We tried very diligently to discuss weather, sports and current events other than the case at hand. Eventually, however, we shared our opinions of the case and discussed them at some length. None of our opinions changed in any way, but it's doubtful our discussion would have been wanted or condoned by the contesting attorneys. As it was, we could just as well have sat in court. Sequestering the witnesses did not serve a useful purpose and risked contaminating the experts' opinions—six hours is a long time.

Eventually, the bailiff arrives in the witness waiting room, asks for you by name and escorts you into court to the court clerk. In the courtroom the court clerk asks you to raise your right hand, place your left hand on the Bible which is provided for you and "solemnly swear" you will "tell the truth, the whole truth, and nothing but the truth, so help you God." You are expected to answer the same way you did when you got married: "I do." Having a sense of humor, I once asked the woman court clerk in a whisper: "Does this mean we're married?" She glared back at me. Court is a very solemn and serious place. I don't recommend "hamming it up," even in a whisper as I did.

The **swearing in** is composed of very powerful words. They are rooted in thousands of years of social evolution, call on the Creator and they are stated publicly as a formal oath. The intent is to deter lying under oath (**perjury**). Taking the oath is for many a moving experience and a solemn occasion. After all, how often do you raise your right hand and "swear on a Bible" to God about anything? Occasionally, there are witnesses whose religious conviction forbids them to swear, or who do not believe in God or scripture. They are allowed to **affirm** rather than to swear, responding to the court clerk's "Do you solemnly swear" with something like, "I do so affirm."

Before you can testify, your attorney facilitates your being **qualified.** Only the judge actually makes this determination. The attorney who requested your testimony "proposes" and the judge "disposes." You will recall that you were identified in the pretrial filings as an expert witness and the opposing attorney has had time to "dig up the dirt" on you, personally and professionally. If your testimony is a serious threat, the attorney will move to have you disqualified, thus eliminating your testimony.

Direct Examination

Direct examination is when "your" attorney asks simple, clear, direct questions to enable you to give your opinion and explain it as needed, such as: "Please state your findings and the methods you used to arrive at them." Attorneys may not ask leading questions of expert witnesses during direct examination. If the opposing counsel thinks your testimony is being shaped by leading questions, s/he will **object** to the judge, saying something like: "Objection, your honor, counsel is leading the witness." The judge then rules the objection is **sustained,** instructing the jury to disregard the question and your answer, or that the objection is **overruled,** allowing the question and your answer to it. Some attorneys lead their witnesses until stopped by a sustained objection. While the jury is to consider the question not asked and the answer not given, the fact is that they were stated and can have an effect on or influence the jury.

Cross-Examination

In some cases, an expert witness can give direct examination and not be cross-examined, but most attorneys will want to review your testimony and try to discount, discredit and raise doubts about it. The opposing attorney has the right to cross-examine you immediately after you have completed your direct examination testimony. Of all court proceedings, it is cross-examination that causes expert witnesses the most discomfort. It has the potential of being the most upsetting aspect of testifying and for many it has left deep and lasting psychological-emotional scars. Cross-examiantion is "open season" for the opposing attorney to pounce on you, first on what you said to lessen its impact on the judge or jury, then on you personally, your tone of voice, attitude, personal traits (sex, race, age, education, religion or social standing). Whatever can be used to discredit your testimony, can and will be used against you if your testimony is a serious threat.

Tactics used in cross-examination are those likely to weaken the weight of your testimony or at worst **impeach** (disqualify) your testimony totally. For example, a minor inconsistency between your pretrial deposition and your trial testimony can be used to suggest you are uncertain or incompetent. If the attorney has a histrionic flair, such a discrepancy can become a personal attack: "There's a difference here in your pretrial and trial testimony and it raises very serious questions about your opinion then and now. Why should there be any difference at all? Were you lying then or are you lying now?" It's an insulting question, humiliating to hear, but perfectly proper in the adversary system of court.

During cross-examination, attorneys can and do ask leading (and loaded) questions. They will probe into the facts and any exceptions to your opinion, turning the probe this way and that, testing or twisting it with hypothetical questions, to try to change the judge or jury's perception to favor their side. For example, in a rape case, the victim can be asked what she wore at the time of the offense, why she was there at the time, even how she walked, makeup or perfume used, to imply that somehow she may have provoked the attack. It can be unkind, even cruel, but remember that the opposing attorney's sworn duty is to represent the client to the best of that attorney's ability. You **are** an expert witness, providing information not otherwise available to the court regardless of the side on which you testify. You should therefore strive to be and to remain truly professional in your attitude, bearing and verbal responses, objective and composed. Because cross-examination can be a formidable obstacle course (with a built-in mine field), it is wise to answer questions with short, simple sentences and in clear, understandable language. This is also a good rule for interrogatories and depositions, since whatever you say can be used against you.

Finally, you should develop a "combat awareness," for in cross-examination "things are seldom what they seem." At a murder trial with full media coverage I was the defendant's only expert witness and I expected the prosecutor to do all he could to disqualify me. So I was prepared for a recitation of credentials "from soup to nuts." I was also quite appehensive, being in the lion's den waiting for the beast to charge. Much to my surprise, he waved his hand and without even looking at me accepted me as an expert witness. After the trial I mentioned to the defense attorney how "nice it was" that the prosecutor so graciously accepted my qualifications. With a patient and indulgent smile, he explained that the prosecutor quickly accepted me to prevent the jury from hearing a detailed account of my qualifications. That would have added weight to my testimony. Without it, I could be (and was!) vigorously cross-examined and if he was successful there would be more weight on his side. His quick acceptance lulled me into a false sense of security which made his later attacks in cross-examination that much more painful to me, a "one-two punch."

Redirect Examination

The attorney who originally called you as an expert witness has the privilege of **recalling** you for **redirect examination.** This is appropriate if new information was developed during cross-examination. It is a tactic to reinstate your expertise, to repair any damage inflicted or recoup anything which might have been lost during cross-examination. For example, if in cross-examination opposing counsel drew you off on a tangent into data and opinions not included in pretrial and direct testimony, these new elements can be further explored by redirect examination. At this stage only information elicited during cross-examination can be discussed.

Recross Examination

Just as cross-examination followed direct examination, so recross-examination follows redirect examination. It enables the opposing attorney to scrutinize your responses in redirect examination and interpret it to support his/her case. While it is rare, in exceptionally complex cases, even more new information may emerge in recross examination. "Your" attorney might then ask for the judge's approval to **re-open direct examination** and the whole process recycles and repeats until both sides are satisfied that all pertinent information is available. Redirect and recross examinations usually occur in cases involving complex technical information.

Rebuttal Evidence

When the defendant's case is concluded, the plaintiff or prosecutor can present **rebuttal evidence.** This is new witness testimony or new evidence not previously presented and it is aimed at refuting defense arguments. It cannot be evidence or a witness previously used in the case, for then it would not be new. It is at this time that a **surprise witness** would be used to good advantage.

Surrebuttal

Surrebuttal is the defense attorney's response to the plaintiff's rebuttal evidence or witness. Whatever has been submitted by the plaintiff is confronted and challenged at this stage.

Closing Arguments

When all of the foregoing examinations have been concluded, each side provides the court with a **summation** of its case. The plaintiff presents first, the defense follows. The summation is the grand overview of the case and includes relevant legal precedents. When finished, the attorney usually says: "The defense (or state) rests."

Verdict

If it is a jury trial the judge will **instruct the jury** as to which verdicts are possible and the grounds necessary to satisfy each of them. If the judge sits alone as trier of fact, then s/he may either announce the decision or recess to take whatever time is necessary to consider the case.

LEGAL REALITIES IN HISTORY AND LITERATURE

Michel Equem de Montaigne (1533-1592) was a French essayist whose writing was a major influence to French and British thought. He was an avid student of Latin classics and he especially liked Plutarch for his analytical insight into leaders past and present and their ideals. Montaigne developed a similar though more skeptical sytle. No stranger to government service and statecraft, he was a courtier to King Charles IX and for four years was mayor of Bordeaux. He provides us with insight into the growing legal philosophy of natural, moral law which eventually crossed the Atlantic to form the American legal justice system.

Montaigne focussed sharply on the issue of law as ideal and law in reality: "Men amuse me when they try to give certainty to our laws by saying that some of them are perpetual and unchangeable which they call 'natural laws.' . . . there is not one of these picked natural laws which is not denounced and disowned by not one nation, but several. . . . One people or another have sanctioned the murder of infants or fathers, community of wives, traffic in robbery and all manner of licentious pleasures." Due to "governing, shuffling and confounding the fact of things" there is a difference between laws "and our capacity to obey them." He concluded, "To set a mark we can seldom hit is not an honest game" (Lowenthal, 1947, p. 355).

Montaigne shifted then his attention from the intent of law to the importance given to precedent: "In a field of learning so illimitable as law, which depends for its authority on multitudinous opinions, and the subject of which is itself so obscure, an endless confusion of decisions must result. One court decides differently from another and on occasion differs from itself" (ibid., p. 358). Montaigne undoubtedly based his opinion on the variability of legal decisionmaking and confusing precedents on his years of observation in the king's court and as mayor of Bordeaux. H. L. Mencken, the **Baltimore Sun** reporter who observed many court cases (most notably, the Scopes "monkey trial") in 1924, summing up a similar opinion: "Injustice is relatively easy to bear; what stings is justice."

Anatole France (1844-1924), French novelist, poet and playwright and 1921 Nobel laureate in literature, was also like Montaigne, a critic and satirist. In his **Crainquebille** he described the unreliability of first-hand descriptions, eyewitness accounts. He reported Sir Walter Raleigh's experience while a prisoner in the Tower of London: "While writing his **History of the World,** he heard a scuffle below his window and looked out to see a fight in the street. The next day a friend visited him who had taken part in that fight. Raleigh was contradicted by his friend on every point. Reflecting, therefore, that if he were mistaken as to events that passed beneath his very eyes, how much greater must be the difficulty in ascertaining the truth concerning events far distant, he threw the manuscript of his history into the fire" (France, 1947, p. 415).

France applied Raleigh's insight to the legal and judicial process: "If judges had the same scruples as Sir Walter Raleigh they would throw all their notes into the fire. But they have no right to do so. They would be thus flouting justice; they would be committing a crime. We may despair of knowing; we must not despair of judging. Those who demand that sentences pronounced in Law Courts should be founded upon a methodical examination of facts are dangerous sophists and perfidious enemies of justice both civil and military" (ibid., p. 415). Samuel Clemens (Mark Twain, 1835-1910) was a contemporary of Anatole France and also had a reputation for his sharp wit and keen insight into human foibles and practical realism. In his **Sketches New and Old** he wrote: "We have a criminal jury system which is superior to any in the world and its efficiency is only marred by the difficulty of finding twelve men every day who don't know anything and can't read."

In 1935, Robert Graves wrote **Claudius the God,** a book about the Roman Emperor Claudius I (10 B.C. - 54 A.D.). He liberalized the laws and he himself served as a magistrate. He has left us his impressions of the experience:

> I detest forensic oratory. If a man cannot state his case in a brief and lucid way, bringing the necessary witnesses and abstaining from irrelevant talk about the nobility of his ancestry, the number of impoverished relatives dependent on him, the clemency and wisdom of the judge, the harsh tricks that fate plays, the mutability of human fortune and all that stale silly bag of tricks, he deserves the extreme penalty of the law for his dishonesty, pretension and his waste of public time (Graves, 1947, p. 329).

Claudius was a strict judge and with very definite views on courtroom procedure. "Often," he wrote, "when I was about to judge a case I used to warn the court with a smile: 'I am an old man and my patience is easily tried. My verdict will probably go to the side that presents its evidence in the briefest, frankest and most lucid manner, even if it is somewhat incriminating, rather than to the side that spoils a good case by putting up an inappropriately brilliant dramatic performance' " (ibid, p. 334). He encourages "a new sort of advocate—men without either eloquence or great legal expertness but with common sense, clear voices and a talent for reducing cases to their simplest elements" (ibid.).

Joseph Addison (1672-1719) served in the British diplomatic service in a variety of positions from undersecretary to Secretary of State. He wrote **The Court of Honor,** a fictitious transcript of the court of "Isaac Bickerstaffe, Esq., Censor of Great Britain." It is a satire on trial procedure, the seemingly trivial details of prosecution, statutes and sentencing. In **Cases of False Delicacy,** a "linen draper" is charged with "speaking obscenely to the Lady Penelope Touchwood" while riding in a public coach with her: "At Knightsbridge he mentioned the word linen; at the further end of Kensington he made use of the term smock; and that before he came to Hammersmith, he talked about a quarter of an hour upon wedding shifts" (Addison, 1947, p. 372).

The lady was agitated and upset by his conversation. The defendant explained "he talked only in his own trade and meant no hurt by what he said. The jury, however, found him guilty." They ruled that "such discourses were apt to sully the imagination and that by a concatenation of ideas the word linen implied many things that were not proper . . . " The jury's verdict was "that the linen draper should lose his tongue." Judge Bickerstaff said the defendant's "ears were as much to blame as the tongue" and "gave sentence as follows: That they should both be placed over against one another in the midst of court, there to remain for the space of one quarter of an hour . . . the linen draper to be gagged and the lady to hold her hands close upon both her ears" (ibid.).

Finley Peter Dunne (1867-1936) was an American humorist who created "Mr. Dooley," an Irish saloon owner and homespun philosopher. In 1907, Standard Oil was fined $29 million in federal court, reversed an appeal. Dooley tells his friend Hinnissy what the judge said: "Ye're an old offender and I'll have to make an example of ye. Twinty-nine million dollars or fifty-eight million days . . . . " Dooley defines an appeal: "An appeal, Hinnissy, is where ye ask one coort to show it's contempt fer another coort." He explains why and how appeals are filed: "Do ye find the larned counsel that's just been beat climbin' up on the bench and throwin' his arms around the judge? Ye bet ye don't. He gathers his law books into his arms, gives the magistrate a look that means 'There's an election next year' and runs down the hall to another judge" (Dunne, 1947, p. 425).

Legal proceedings and court procedures are so complex that cases can be tried, recessed, continued and appealed for years. Statutes have loopholes which can delay or avoid resolving conflict. In his **Critical Essay upon the Faculties of the Mind** (1707), Jonathan Swift wrote that "laws are like cobwebs which may catch small flies but let wasps and hornets break through." Clarence Darrow (1857-1938), one of America's most famous trial lawyers with an impressive record of successes in difficulty cases, said in 1936: "There is no such thing as justice—in or out of court."

When two experienced, forceful and persuasive attorneys spar at each other with an array of evidence and witnesses on both sides, it appears there is more than one truth. What may have seemed clear at the trial's beginning becomes more clouded as the two sides argue. It is the verbal equivalent to the immovable object meeting the irresistible force. Luigi Pirandello described the effect of the direct confrontation of two very nearly equal forces: "Truth is what you think it is at any given time." This raises questions as to the nature of truth, the difficulty of ever knowing "the truth, the whole truth and nothing but the truth." Alfred North Whitehead (1861-1947), world-renowned philosopher and mathematician and Harvard Professor, maintained that "there are no whole truths; all truths are half-truths. It is trying to treat them as whole truths that plays the devil" (**Dialogues,** 1953, p. 16).

There was that man, Socrates, and he was tried, convicted and executed by a jury of his peers. His truth and the jury's truth were not the same. Both sides remained true to their ideals. Neither yielded. Plato—Socrates's loyal student—carefully took down his teacher's words. They reflect an extraordinary awareness of the strengths and weaknesses of the adversary system of our courts:

> How you have felt, O men of Athens, at hearing the speeches of my accusers I cannot tell, but I know that their persuasive words almost made me forget who I was, such was the effect of them, and yet they have hardly spoken a word of truth. But many as their falsehoods were there was one of them which quite amazed me. I mean when they told you to be upon your guard and not to let yourself be deceived by the force of my eloquence. They ought to have been ashamed of saying this because they were sure to be detected as soon as I opened my lips and displayed my deficiency; they certainly did appear to be most shameless in saying this unless by the force of my eloquence they mean the force of truth, for then I do indeed admit that I am eloquent. But in how different a way from theirs! (Eliot, 1909)

Socrates going calmly to his death, Antigone's defense of her illegal burial of her brother, the other cases and quotes in these pages, trace the evolution of due process. It is doubtful Socrates or Antigone would be convicted today. Even if they were, there would be an appeals system in place and more legal precedents to moderate any sentences imposed. With pretrial conferences, plea bargaining, state and federal appeals courts and other similar procedures, we may have veered to the left. "The quality of mercy is not strained," Shakespeare wrote in **The Merchant of Venice** (1596), "it droppeth as the gentle rain from heaven upon the place beneath; it is twice blessed, it blesseth him that gives and him that takes and 'tis mightiest in the mightiest . . ." We are a mighty nation and much of that might involves our mercy.

This chapter introduces cold reality to the warmth and idealism of Chapter 2. In practice the adversary system may seem crude, impersonal and upsetting. Every day newspapers and TV news offer many examples of apparent injustice in a court somewhere. Focussing only on them leads to the cynicism and sarcasm of the writers quoted in this chapter. To judge the legal and judicial system by this limited sampling is unfair and incorrect. The vast majority of cases fulfill the high ideals of Chapter 2. The "bad cases" are the exceptions, not the rule.

Despite sometimes harsh realities we still have the best legal system the world has ever produced—because it has come from the world, from time immemorial. If you've had a bad day in court, or doubt we've made much progress in the pursuit of truth and justice, reread Chapter 2 and skip this chapter, except for these words of John Stuart Mill (1806-1873) from his essay **On Liberty**:

> If all mankind, minus one, were of one opinion, and only one person was of the contrary opinion, mankind would be no more justified in silencing that one person than he, if he had the power, would be justified in silencing mankind. Wrong opinions and practices gradually yield to fact and argument; but facts and arguments, to produce any effect on the mind, must be brought before it. Very few facts are able to tell their own story without comments to bring out their meaning . . . . Not the violent conflict between parts of the truth but the quiet suppression of half of it—that is the formidable evil. There is always hope when people are forced to listen to both sides; it is only when they attend only to one that errors harden into prejudices and truth itself ceases to have the effect of truth by being exaggerated into falsehood (Leavens, 1941, p. 546).

REFERENCES

Addison, J. (1947). Two hearings before Isaac Bickerstaffe. In A. Curiae (Ed.), *Law in action: An anthology of the law in literature.* New York: Bonanza Books.

American Bar Association (1980). *Law and the courts.* Chicago: Author.

Dunne, F. P. (1947). The big fine. In A. Curiae (Ed.), *Law in action: An anthology of the law in literature.* New York: Bonanza Books.

Eliot, C. W. (Ed.) (1909). *The apology, Phaedo and Crito of Plato* (Jewett translation). In the Harvard Classics, Volume 2. New York: P. F. Collier, page 3.

Fielding, H. (1947), Jonahtan Thrusher, Esq., Justice of the peace, deals with sundry affairs. In A. Curiae (Ed.), *Law in action: An anthology of the law in literature.* New York: Bonanza Books.

France, A. (1947). Crainqueville. In A. Curiae (Ed.), *Law in action: An anthology of law in literature.* New York: Bonanza Books.

Graves, R. (1947). Crainqueville. In A. Curiae (Ed.), *Law in action: An anthology of law in literature.* New York: Bonanza Books.

Leavens, R. F. (Ed.) (1941). *Great companions: Readings on the meaning and conduct of life from ancient and modern sources.* Volumes I and II. Boston: Beacon Press.

Lowenthal, M. (Trans.) (1947). A magistrate of Bordeaux: Michel de Montaigne. In A. Curiae (Ed.), *Law in action: An anthology of law in literature.* New York: Bonanza Books.

CHAPTER 4

LAWYERING

If you read something
you can't understand,
you can be sure
a lawyer wrote it!
—Will Rogers

LAWYERS are called by many names: attorney, advocate, legal representative, litigator, even champion and gladiator. Depending on your interaction and experience with them, you may think of them in other terms. It has been my experience that as a group they are not unlike any other profession. As individuals, they are people you like or dislike as you would neighbors, co-workers or family members and this is not at all unusual. They are a cross section of personalities and attitudes. Some you would choose as a friend, others not so. This chapter is intended to acquaint you with what all attorneys share in common: their obligation to defend their client regardless of the charges or notoriety attached to the case.

It is difficult for the non-lawyer public to understand the duties and responsibilities binding on attorneys by the adversary system and their own professional code of ethics. Many critics contend that attorneys are not interested in "the whole truth" but only that part of the truth that supports their case. Saks and Hastie (1978) maintain "that it is not the advocate's role to be fair and balanced and to do so would be harmful to the search for truth" (p. 205). Legal truth emerges from the pitched verbal battle between defendant and plaintiff, observed and judged by impartial "triers of fact" (judges and juries). "It is the system that produces truth, not its constituent elements . . . [or] from well-intentioned seekers of truth" (Saks & Hastie, 1978, p. 206).

LAW V. SCIENCE

Law and science seek truth in much the same way. Both have rules of evidence and make judgments as to what is true (Kurke, 1986). For science, professional books and journals are the "court of opinion" where new discoveries are made and older ones retested. The rise and fall of theories is reflected in the scientific literature much as changing legal precedents and appelate court decisions affect the practice of law. William James (1842-1910), psychologist, philosopher, and founder of pragmatism, held that the adversary system of law was like science where "competing theories are tested by biased proponents." One great difference, of course, is that there is a judge or jury in the legal process which decides truth in every case.

Both law and psychology are deeply involved in aspects of human behavior. Both seek to answer the question: "What's normal?" Psychology wants to know **what, how and why** we behave as we do; law wants to know what **should be** our behavior. Psychology is statistical and normative in its search for truth. Law is historical (statutes), archival (precedents) and proscriptive, defining what actions are not to be tolerated. "Psychology asks what measure can and should be taken to enable the deviant to function more effectively, while law seeks to determine what measures shall be taken to remedy the consequence of deviation . . . " (Kurke, 1986, p. 223).

There are other differences between law and the sciences. Law is clearly and intentionally adversarial, seeking to vindicate only one of the two sides. Science is collegial and many sided, a more open forum where any and all hypotheses can be tested. Law as reflected in a given case is final; there is a decision one way or the other. Science is a continuing process which rarely "finishes" with anything. In this sense, law is limited (by statute and precedent) and a closed system. Science is less limited and more of an open system. The law looks for truth in sharp black-and-white focus and it wants to know what's true in the specific case at hand. Science sees truth as "a many splendored thing," with many facets—it wants to know them all.

These differences explain why attorneys and expert witnesses often have difficulty communicating even when they use the same words. Both seemingly agree to seek "the truth, the whole truth and nothing but the truth" and both speak of "evidence." In practice, however, there are differences in the education, training and working realities between law and other professions. There is a difference in basic attitude and this causes behavioral differences in court.

For example, attorneys are trained never to ask a question for which they do not already know the answer or all possible answers. They build algorithms, channeling all possible answers to conclusions to favor their own case. They are trained to carefully research each case, to nitpick into what may seem trivia, for exceptions, inconsistencies, contradictions. These will be emphasized. In my experience, most attorneys will first go after your opinion, then your credentials, then you personally. If attacked on all three of these fronts, accept it as a compliment. It means your testimony is perceived as important enough to require such a concerted attack.

Here are some examples of other courtroom strategies frequently used by attorneys:

Shaping Truth

Attorneys can, by the questions they ask, limit the information provided and in this way control and shape what judge and jury perceive as the truth. Expert witnesses provide information not otherwise available, and if even this is limited and controlled, triers of fact have less information on which to base their findings. In some cases, courtroom procedures and rules of evidence can be used to control expert witness testimony despite an aware and vigorously opposing attorney.

Half Truth

Alfred Lord Tennyson (1809-1892) described this technique in **The Grandfather** written in 1864: "A lie which is all lie may be met and fought with outright but a lie which is part a truth is a harder matter to fight." A clever attorney can state and restate an issue or "fact" which is almost true until all of it seems true. "For a moment the lie becomes truth," Fedor Dostoevski (1821-1881) wrote, a year before his death, in the epilog to **The Brothers Karamazov** (1880). It's an old propaganda device, endlessly repeating your truth until it becomes **the** truth. Another aspect of the half-truth is a **half-error**—when a false statement contains some truth. Henry Frederic Amiel (1821-1881) wrote in his **Journal** in 1883: "An error is more dangerous the more truth it contains."

A variation of the half truth technique is to deliberately withhold all the truth. Once upon a time there was a car-train accident at a railroad crossing at midnight. The railroad was sued for negligence, for giving insufficient warning at the uncontrolled crossing. There was a night watchman on the scene and the opposing attorney grilled him in detail from visibility ("It was pitch black") to his every movement ("I stood in the middle of the crossing in plain view and held the lantern up above my head and I waved it back and forth"). The railroad won. After the trial, the watchman confided to the railroad attorney: "I'm damn glad he didn't ask me if the lantern was lit" (Buescher, 1984, pp. 159-160).

Exceptions

This is a frequently used strategy, perhaps the most used in all of law. It is Olympic-quality nit-picking, sifting through all the material and separating out isolated incidents or exceptions to the general rule. The subject doesn't matter. Attorneys using this device usually ask questions beginning with: "Is it **always** true that? . . . " Sometimes, a hypothetical question is asked based on an exception to your testimony or an exception to a general rule of practice. A hypothetical question is an effective way for an opposing attorney to discover exceptions and then use them. Actually, this is an ancient practice described 2,000 years ago by our old friend Aristotle (384-322 B.C.): "The least initial deviation from the truth is multiplied later a thousandfold" (**On the Heavens,** Book 1, verse 5).

Exceptions can be a very sensitive and difficult subject for expert witnesses, since, as Socrates pointed out, "The more you know, the more you realize you don't know." There are exceptions to just about every rule. We are urged by judges and legal experts to keep our expert witnesses testimony clear and simple, to avoid specialized vocabulary and jargon. When we do so, we depart from precision and move into the larger world of semantics, where the same words can have several meanings. Here's an example of how clear and simple language can be used to question an expert's credibility:

Attorney:	In your opinion, will the sun rise tomorrow?
Expert:	Yes. (or s/he could say) Since the earth rotates West to East the morning sun will be seen as rising on the Eastern horizon.

Which answer is best? The first, a simple "yes" **tracks** you. You will probably be encouraged to respond to future questions with "yes" or "no." The second answer is more scientific, more objective. But to many it can sound like "jargon," unduly complicated. I recommend the second, though if you can phrase it in even simpler language, so much the better.

The attorney asking the questions might even say so, just to try to "channel" you into "yes" or "no"—that's what's on the algorithm chart to lead you into contradictory or inconsistent testimony. Would you believe that either way you're in a trap? Let's see!

Attorney: Thank you, Sir (or Ma'am). That's certainly a very clear and concise answer (believe that and I got a special deal for you on a bridge in Brooklyn!). Let us suppose it is overcast and raining in the morning, what then?

Expert: My answer then is yes and no. Yes, the sun will rise for the reasons I've already stated, and no it would not be seen at that time because of the local weather conditions.

Not a bad answer, still scientific and objective. The mistake the expert is making is accepting the attorney's frame of reference and language. The attorney could "nail" you now with an attack such as: "I suggest to you that it cannot be that the sun can rise and not rise, that a scientific fact can and cannot be at one and the same time. I suggest to you that your approach in all of your testimony in this case carries with it the same flaw. Inconsistent, contradictory (and if the attorney wants to throw in the kitchen sink and punch below the belt) and an insult to the intelligence of this court." Let's play it out a bit longer.

Attorney: Is it not true (a favorite sentence start) that it is firmly established scientific fact (you're in trouble when you hear this wording) that the sun does not "rise" at all but is fixed in our solar system, the earth rotating around it?

Expert: Yes.

Now you're in the attorney's "funnel" headed for the sewer! Notice, there's much less room to explain your answer. It's as if you're flying down a valley between two mountain ranges unable to fly over them and with less and less space in which to turn around.

Attorney: Sir/Ma'am, I put it to you (as the British say), would it not be as logical to say the EARTH rises?

You're off and running. The language has been twisted around and regardless of how you answer **you** are going to sound inconsistent, contradictory or confused. Notice, too, that the sun's rising doesn't have anything to do with anything. It illustrates the point that a clever attorney can introduce any subject to an expert witness and use it to diminish credibility or worse still impeach or disqualify the witness.

Attorneys use this technique as described here, based on subjects they introduce minimally or tangentially related to the case. They then refer back to your previous answers and show how you contradicted yourself on "important basic facts" which "raise serious concerns about your credibility." If the "streetfighter" type, they may throw in other choice comments such as: "Were you confused then or are you confused now?" It can be more dangerous if it can be shown that your present testimony contradicts your responses to interrogatories or depositions. I've had attorneys attempt to use quotations from my own published articles to contradict my trial testimony. The writings were general, my testimony specific to the case, so this strategy didn't pay off.

Ralph Waldo Emerson (1803-1882) described the great difficulty in defining truth, since whenever you forthrightly state it, exceptions or opposite truths emerge: "It is the fault of our rhetoric that we cannot strongly state one fact without seeming to belie some other" (**Essays, First Series,** 1841).

LAWYER JOKES

The lay public's lack of awareness of why attorneys do what they do has led to bias and ridicule, reflected in Will Rogers's cynical comment which opened this chapter. "Lawyer jokes" are a further example of how the public does not really know or appreciate attorneys' duties which are inherent in the due process of law. Attorneys push, sometimes hard, to prove their case. If they did not do so, truth and justice would be diminished. Truth shines brightly despite the direct confrontation of the adversary system. "Fraud and falsehood dread examination," Thomas Cooper wrote, "but truth invites it."

This basic idea has been stated in other ways: "It is better to debate a question without settling it than to settle it without debate" (Joseph Joubet); "you can't thoroughly understand a truth until you have contended against it" (Ralph Waldo Emerson). As it proceeds, the legal and trial process can wear away patience, and verbal combat can erode self-esteem. "You should never wear your best trousers when you go out to fight for freedom and truth," Henrik Ibsen (1826-1906) aptly observed in act V of his play, **An Enemy of the People** (1882). William Penn, founder of Pennsylvania, a haven for the religiously oppressed, wrote in 1683 that "it is endless to dispute upon everything that is disputable" (Some Fruits of Solitude). "The dignity of truth is lost with much protesting," Ben Jonson (1572-1637) wrote in act III, scene 2 of his play **Cataline's Conspiracy.** Thomas Jefferson (1743-1826), ever the champion of truth, justice and the ideal of due process, contended that "reason and free inquiry are the only effectual agents against error."

To the lay public, legal proceedings can seem endless and the points in contention unimportant and trivial. The attorneys and judge seem to know what's going on and act as if it's all very important, but at the same time the jury may be "on the nod," dozing off. Dick Cavett, TV talk show host, described such proceedings as "the bland leading the bland." Carl Sandburg (1936) wrote of a twentieth century lawyer who said of another lawyer "he has one of the most enlightened minds of the eighteenth century" (p. 182). Michel de Montaigne (1533-1592) observed that while "no one is exempt from talking nonsense, the mistake is to do it solemnly." If a defense attorney is a vigorous advocate, s/he might be called "a hired gun." If a vigorous prosecutor, the epithet might be "executioner" or "hangman." If the attorney is neither, the name-calling can be "bland" or even "incompetent."

Because of this basic misunderstanding and consequent mistrust, attorneys have been the subject of many jokes. Here's a sampler:

An anonymous humorist defined a lawyer as "a person in whom ignorance of the law goes unpunished." Another jokester reports this dialogue as an attorney nears death: "He's lying at death's door," one observer says, and another adds: "He's at death's door and he's still lying?" Then there's the story that Saint Peter and the Devil had a dispute over the border between Heaven and Hell. St. Peter threatened to sue and the Devil laughed heartily, commenting: "Oh yea? Where you gonna get a lawyer?" Judge Braude tells of this dialogue between attorney and client: "When I was a boy," the lawyer said, "I always wanted to be a pirate." The client replied: "Congratulations!" (Braude, 1964, p. 160). Walt Buescher (1984) described a heated exchange between opposing attorneys: "You're a liar!" one attorney shouted. "And you're a crook!" his adversary countered. The judge, unruffled, calmly observed: "Now that counsel have introduced themselves, let us proceed" (pp. 7-8). Clarence Darrow told the story of a doctor in a malpractice case who protested to the opposing attorney: "Your profession doesn't make angels of us." The attorney replied: "No sir, you doctors have us there." Carl

Sandburg wrote a dialogue in 1936 where a newcomer to town asks: "Have you a criminal lawyer in this burg?" The reply: "We think so but we haven't been able to prove it on him" (p. 154).

An attorney, a clergyman and a psychiatrist were shipwrecked, floating on a raft of debris. After many days adrift they spot land, but there are sharks circling around them. The clergyman says: "I have faith and my religion will save me from harm." He jumps overboard, swims a few feet, and is eaten by the sharks. The psychiatrist says: "The sharks have eaten now and my understanding of their behavior will save me." He jumps over and is eaten by the sharks. Alone and with no other hope, the attorney jumps into the sea and much to his surprise the sharks line up on either side of him and escort him to shore. Safely on the beach, he shouts his thanks to the sharks and asks: "But why?" In a chorus, the sharks reply: "Professional courtesy!"

This one's a riddle: One day the devil, a low-fee attorney and a high-fee attorney are walking down the street. On the pavement in front of them is a one-dollar bill. Which of the three picked it up? The high-fee attorney, of course, because the other two are fictitious!

Attorneys are not the only subjects (or victims) of law jokes. Judges and juries are not immune. An anonymous author has defined a jury as "twelve people who vote who has the best lawyer." In Chapter 3 we heard Mark Twain's opinion that the great difficulty with juries is "finding twelve men every day who don't know anything and can't read." As for judges, the story is told that a witness was asked what the defendant said at the time of the alleged offense. The witness replied: "It isn't fit to tell a gentleman." The attorney replied: "Well, then, whisper it in the judge's ear." Carl Sandburg (1936) offered this tongue-in-cheek definition of a judge:

> What is a judge? One . . . coming to his decisions often in a blur of hesitations knowing by what snarled courses and ropes of reason justice operates, with reservations, in twilight zones (**The people, yes**, p. 188).

LAWYERS IN HISTORY

As we have seen in Chapter 2, law is an ancient, hallowed tradition, called "the second oldest profession" by some. Curiae (1947) traces the growth of law as we know it today to the Middle Ages, when Italian universities revived the study of Roman law. The "great offices of state" were held by the clergy. Even at the height of the **Protestant Reformation** there was opposition to attorneys processing conflict: "At the Reformation, theological objections to law and lawyers were about the only thing on which Roman Catholic and Reformer were agreed" (Curiae, 1947, p. xi). Montaigne (1947) reported that "King Ferdinand wisely provided that no lawyers could join in the new colonies sent to America, lest lawsuits should get a footing in the new world: he agreed with Plato that 'lawyers and doctors are the pests of a country' " (p. 357).

Anatole France (1844-1924) wrote about the transition between divine and civil law, clergy to lawyer. In his humorous work, **Cranquebille,** the story of a citizen tried for insulting a policeman, he describes the rise of civil law after the **French Revolution**:

> Over the tribune were a bust representing the Republic and a crucifix, as if to indicate that all laws divine and human were suspended over Cranquebille's head. Such symbols naturally inspired him with terror. Not being gifted with a philosophic mind, he did not inquire the bust and the crucifix; he did not ask how far Jesus and the symbolical bust harmonized in the Law Courts. Nevertheless, here was matter for reflection; for, after all, pontifical teaching and canon law are in many points opposed to the constitution of the Republic and to the civil code . . . . Today, as formerly, the Church of Christ teaches that only those powers are lawful to which it has given its sanction. Now the French Republic claims to be independent of pontifical power" (France, 1947, p. 407).

In Seventeenth century colonial America, "the clergy were supreme. Legal practice emerged as a major profession in the mid-eighteenth century and by 1800: executive justice and legislative justice which had prevailed in the colonial period were definitely superseded by judicial justice" (ibid. pp. xii-xiii). By the **Civil War,** common law, a blend of Old English case and statutory law, was integrated into the American legal and judicial systems. Attorneys gradually assumed more responsibility for and participated more in the legal process, from the clergy-dominated Puritans in isolated settlements, the frontier justice of sheriffs and marshalls in small towns to the application of local, state and federal laws coast to coast. The rise of the legal profession in the United States duplicates the rise of the nation itself.

LAWYERING TODAY

In 1960 there were 286,000 attorneys in the United States, one for every 627 people. In 1986 there were 700,000 attorneys, one for every

354 (Sullivan, 1986). Of these, 100,000 of them started practice within the last five years. There are more lawyers in the United States than any other nation in the world. In 1966, 70,906 suits were filed in federal courts. In 1986, 254, 828 federal cases were filed (Kester, 1987). There are a flood of new statutes passed every year (about 400 annually for Congress) and each of the 50 state legislatures do their own. Law is a business and a profession and the statistics show that business is brisk—but the number of attorneys seeking a share in it is also at an unprecedented high level. The net result is that the adversary system is very much alive and well.

LAWYER TYPES

Attorneys are people and that means there is a great variety of personality types and interpersonal communications styles among them. At the risk of oversimplification but based on a decade of courtroom experience, the following six basic lawyer types are described. I've met them all, in the United States and Canada, in courts at every level. It is as if there is an international brotherhood/sisterhood or a kind of family of attorney types. My object in describing them is not to deprecate the legal profession but to help you adjust to and cope with attorneys in court. Some attorneys may combine the traits of more than one of these five. Some may not have a sufficiently distinctive style to perfectly fit any of them.

The Surgeon

In my experience this is a frequently encountered attorney type. They are painstakingly thorough and very effective. If you can relax enough, it's fascinating to watch them work, methodically building their case. Like experienced, effective surgeons, they are aware and alert, attentive to detail and to what is happening at every moment. They "never miss a trick." As you testify in your direct examination they listen intently to every word, observing you carefully. In cross-examination they systematically and meticulously probe and cut through to the heart of your testimony. They have a sharply honed, well-developed skill in accumulating, sifting and selecting the most relevant information, put and keep it in perspective, then apply it expertly to present their case. They deftly "put you to the test" so that you know without any doubt you've wrestled with "a pro, a heavyweight." Regardless of the anxiety or frustration you may experience at their hands, these surgeon-attorneys impress you. The highest compliment I've heard about them comes from judges, jurors, other attorneys, expert witnesses and court spectators, most typically: "If I ever need an attorney, s/he is the one I'd call first, no doubt about it."

Ole Yeller

These attorneys are very loud and forceful, bellicose and barking. The males have a "Superdad" booming, resonating voice; the females have a voice of higher pitch but not shrill, equally as commanding as the males and with a definite "Supermom" quality. They "stand tall," overbearing and superior. I've seen them stand in court, hands on hips, foot tapping, and looking at witnesses the same way a parent looks at little Johnny or Janie caught in the act, hand in the cookie jar. They like to hear themselves and so they tend to look up and out, listening for their voices to echo back and fill the room. They tend to have a histrionic flair and like to gesture, to point with their finger at documents, charts or in your face. They like to handle objects dramatically, abruptly closing books or tossing papers on to the tabletop. Male "barkers" like to use their deeper, booming voices like a weapon. Female "barkers" usually have a sharp, cutting voice due to its being higher in pitch. Carl Sandburg (1936) left us an apt description of **Ole Yellers**:

> "If the law is against you, talk about the evidence," said a battered barrister. "If the evidence is against you, talk about the law and, since you ask me, if the law and the evidence are both against you, then pound the table and yell like hell" (p. 181).

The most frequent reaction of expert witnesses subjected to barkers is to feel "talked down to" (that's because you are!). Sensitive witnesses are likely to be "easily rattled" because the "barker" can hook into childhood memories of being humiliated by a parent or relative. I've had barker attorneys lean in close to me so carried away they were trembling, red-faced and yelling so actively they were spitting on me! I continued speaking calmly and slowly removed my pocket handkerchief and mopped my face (not my forehead which might have misled the barker he was getting to me). He backed off still barking—I do believe there's a barking instinct in them somewhere, a bonafide genetic trait.

The antidote for a barker's "bite" is to do your "matador routine" which is to calmly sidestep the charging beast. When the barking starts, check yourself out, put on your imaginary matador outfit and prepare to stand up and above the attacks. Like their canine cousins, courtroom barkers don't bite. Never bark back. One mad dog in court is quite enough! It's not wise to compete, anyway. They'd just bark longer and, if antagonized, louder. That's their style and they've been doing it a long time. Keep in mind that when Ole Yeller is on the courtroom stage it's the fourth of July, a dramatic performance.

They are the attorney types who are most likely to attack you personally, for how you speak rather than what you say. Stay cool, don't compete, and use your normal, relaxed tone of voice and comfortable, appropriate speed of delivery, and rational and responsible behavior to contrast against the beast's ranting and raving. While undergoing this humiliation (that's pretty much what it is), it might be helpful to remind yourself that it's "be-kind-to-dumb-animals week."

Sweetheart

These attorneys are friendly and ingratiating, like the proverbial guy or the gal next door. Psychologically, they may remind you of someone in your past or present life you feel very comfortable with, a trusted friend or relative. It may be body chemistry. If the two of you had met under other circumstances, you'd probably hit it off like long lost friends or lovers. Interacting with them in court is much like a shipboard romance. They have a great deal of personal charm, a warm and friendly manner. You can't help but like them. They tend to speak softly and look deeply into your eyes. Many expert witnesses confide later that they felt very uncomfortable being "examined" by Sweetheart attorneys. Imagine a seduction plot—you're in one! They are positively disarming—which is precisely the object.

The antidote against Sweethearts is to preserve your virginity! The first step is early detection that this person is getting "close" to you and then is trying to get "inside," into your confidence so that you lower your guard. S/he then "feeds you a line" in the form of a hypothetical question or situation, half-truth or open-ended leading question. That's the seduction. If you submit (agree), you lose credibility. Use the same defenses you would for a used car salesperson, a religious zealot, or smooth con artist. The sweetheart is a combination of all these. They can be very smooth. Sweetheart opposing attorneys are **not** your friends.

Speedy Gonzalez

Speedy Gonzalez attorneys are always in a hurry—intentionally so. They are experts at rapid-fire questions giving you little time to think and reflect on your answers. The effect of this machine gun delivery is to raise your anxiety level and decrease your thinking time and therefore your ability to answer thoughtfully. They usually supplement their speed with looks or sounds of impatience to give the judge or jury the impression your answers are not clear or to the point, that you are being evasive or devious.

If you allow yourself to be manipulated in this way, your mental processes so accelerated, it is almost certain you will lose to these attorneys. It is very unlikely you can match their speed and keep pace with them and even if you did they know the territory and the map as to where it's all heading. You'd have to think and speak quickly and at the same time try to figure out their objective. That puts you at a disadvantage. The antidote for Speedy Gonzalez is to slow down your responses. Pause slightly before answering questions (which you should be doing anyway). Use "braking words" such as: "In my opinion that would be generally true if . . . . " But don't be evasive (can backfire, arouses suspicion, you're talking like an attorney). If you are confronted with words such as "Why do you hesitate? Aren't you sure of the answer?" try responding with something like "These are important questions and I want to think them through before answering." Coping tactics are discussed at greater length in Chapter 6.

The Ole Philosopher

These attorneys are full of homespun humor or earthy wisdom and use quaint figures of speech. They like to tell jokes, quote proverbs and poetry, and self-disclose "homey" details of their own life. They use humor effectively as a weapon, moving judge and jury to laugh about something really funny, then and if successful, ending with laughing at you. They can move off tangentially (or so it seems) into abstract ideas or into the arts. They tend to put themselves down, but by "turn of a phrase" you end up being put down further. There is much method to their madness. They're the foxes of the legal profession.

These attorneys can get and keep you thoroughly confused. You know your area of expertise and they talk around it, seemingly in circles with little relevance to your testimony. They are experts at laying verbal traps, concealed in the brush and in the fog of their verbiage. The antidote against **the Ole Philosopher** is to smile with them but keep your brain cells firing, or in the words of Oliver Cromwell "Trust in God but keep your powder dry." Watch for the kicker. There's bound to be one.

Don't compete with them by trying to match stories and jokes. They have a larger repertoire and know better how and why they're using them.

The Streetfighter

These are vicious, unscrupulous "anything goes" attorneys, the muckrakers of the legal profession. Their specialty is character assassination. They "dig up dirt" and use it. To them, the end justifies any means and they will discredit expert witnesses on personal rather than professional grounds, such as: marriage or family therapists because they've been married several times; relatively low grades or flunked exams of psychologists, psychiatrists or physicians; minor alcohol, drug, or traffic offenses many years past.

The effect of a Streetfighter's personal attack can be devastating, especially if it is sudden and unexpected. There will be little or no opportunity to reply, depending on whether or not the attorney requesting your testimony intervenes to object or clarifies later. The antidote is to retain (or regain) your composure and your dignity. Plug in your "matador defense" described previously. If the **ad hominen** (personal) attacks have nothing at all to do with your testimony or the case, that fact alone may be obvious to the judge and/or jury. Some legal experts say that character assassination in court is not effective (Keeton, 1973). In my opinion "it's all relative" and an unanswered personal attack may "stick" in the minds of a jury. Certainly, it is a more negative than positive influence. If you are "done in" by a Streetfighter, reflect on these words of Norman Vincent Peale: "Twist the truth and make a hit; tell the truth and get hit."

Alan Dershowitz (1982), practicing attorney, legal scholar and professor of law (Harvard), describes seven types of lawyers he has "represented or encountered" in his practice (p. 384-417). While his observations are based only on criminal lawyers, in my opinion the attitudes and behaviors he describes can apply to other specialties of law:

"The Criminal Lawyer Who Gets in Bed with the Clients."

Here, Dershowitz refers to attorneys who become associates, partners or stockholders in their clients' businesses. It is a basic conflict of interest, "the result of a temptation to which lawyers—some good and some not so good—all too often fall prey: they fail to draw a line between representing a client and becoming his associate" (p. 385).

"The Media-Oriented Defense Lawyer"

These are attorneys who attempt to manipulate or influence the court through media publicity. This is the opposite of the grounds for **change of venue,** when the attorney charges a local jury may be prejudiced against the defendant because of undue or widespread publicity. Dershowitz points out with examples how media "hype" can backfire and is at best unpredictable in its effect.

"The Criminal Lawyer Who Serves as 'House Counsel' for Professional Criminals"

These attorneys are frequently portrayed in the movies. The danger is that in time law enforcement agencies and courts identify the attorney with the criminal client. The effect is to "target" these attorneys for possible charges themselves. "A law degree," Dershowitz maintains, "is not a license to join criminal enterprises" (p. 400).

"The Prosecutor in Defense Attorney's Clothing"

These are attorneys with a bias toward the prosecution even when they represent defendants. "They may look like defense attorneys," Dershowitz observes and "they may talk like defense attorneys. They may even have defendants as clients. But they are really prosecutors at heart" (p. 400). Some are former prosecuting attorneys who "hope some day to return to the prosecutorial establishment." They have a "friendship with the current prosecutors" and use it to get "the best possible deal for the client" but this can involve remaining "in the good graces of the current prosecutor even at the expense of a particular client" (p. 402).

"The Perry Mason Lawyers"

These emulate Perry Mason of TV fame, a "clever strategist subtly weaving a psychological net . . . . " In the real world Dershowitz says "such stratagems generally backfire. Cross-examination rarely succeeds in getting the witness to admit that he lied." Attorneys must know when **not** to cross-examine, "when to leave well enough, or even bad enough alone." Dershowitz describes a murder case where no corpse was found. In his closing argument the "Perry Mason" defense attorney announced the alleged victim would "walk through the courtroom door" when he counted to ten. He counted and the eyes of the jurors "riveted upon the door." No one entered. He smiled and commented: "See, each of you turned your eyes to the door. You each must have had a reasonable doubt" that the alleged victim was really dead. The jury **convicted** the defendant. Bewildered, the attorney asked a juror why the conviction. "We all looked at the door," the juror explained, "but we noticed the defendant did not. He knew nobody was going to walk through it."

"Integrity Lawyers"

These are "the good ole boys" of the legal profession, "elder statesmen" and "fairhaired boys" frequently at the top of eligibility lists for judges. They are "distinguished lawyers who see themselves as above the fray." They tend to "argue in unemotional tones" and "would never dream of using a strategem or trick no matter how essential to their client's case." They tend to place their reputation and standing in the legal community "above the immediate needs of the Client" (pp. 404-405).

"The Defense Attorney Who Places Causes Before Clients"

This is the knight in shining armor who champions a cause and uses clients (and others) as a means to the end. The cause may be police brutality, capital punishment, child abuse, women's rights, pro- or anti-abortion, racial injustice, Bill of Rights, you name it and there's a Don Quixote or Sir Lancelot out there, mounted, sword in hand, eager and ready. Dershowitz observes that "their causes may be noble but each can at least on occasion conflict with the interests of a particular client in a specific case" (p. 406).

"Overzealous and Underzealous Defense Attorneys"

Dershowitz describes a polarity of overdoing and underdoing. He confesses to being overzealous himself, is aware of this, and recommends it over the opposite extreme: "The best defense may often be a vigorous and zealous offense" (p. 414). He characterizes underzealous attorneys as being "simply lazy . . . their primary concern is in disposing of the case as quickly as possible so that they can take new cases and earn new fees" (p. 410).

"The Best and the Worst Defense Attorneys"

"The best defense attorneys," Dershowitz maintains, "will always be those who are able to adapt their styles and techniques to the needs of a particular client at a given time." He offers rules for selecting "the best defense attorney." Be certain the attorney serves the best interests of the client and not "some other personal or professional interest" (media exposure, enhanced reputation, pro-prosecution, judgeship, etc.). The ideal attorney should have "a diverse array of weapons . . a lawyer for all seasons." Those to avoid: "the lazy or busy lawyer who simply fails to devote sufficient time or energy to the case; the lawyer who makes the same 'canned' arguments without regard to the facts or law of the case; the lawyer who neglects to preserve pretrial and trial errors for appelate review" (p. 414). Dershowitz concludes: "The zealous defense attorney is the last bastion of liberty, the final barrier between an overreaching government and its citizens." They "challenge the government to make those in power justify their conduct in relation to the powerless."

PRAIRIE LAWYER

There was a self-taught young man who studied for and passed the bar exams in Illinois more than a hundred years ago. He and his law partners wrote about his experience as an attorney. His name was Abraham Lincoln, and the following anecdotes and quotes are taken from a chapter "Prairie Lawyer" in Carl Sandburg's 1926 book, **The Prairie Years,** as reprinted in Curiae (1974). They are offered here to conclude this chapter which has traced the development of law from colonial times to the present. Its strengths and its weaknesses have been described by its champions and by its critics. In many ways, Abe Lincoln, the attorney, is a characterization of what "lawyering" is all about.

In the 1850s, Abe Lincoln was a trial lawyer living with his wife in a corner house in Springfield, Illinois. The pavements were wooden planks, the streets largely unpaved, and horses, carriages and feet were the everyday means of transport. He was the same great man history would later recognize, but neither he nor the people he dealt with knew it then. Gas lights were newly installed and as a matter of fact, Lincoln certified the title of the local gasworks lot. Railroads were expanding from Chicago to the Mississippi River, threatening the lucrative paddlewheel steamer trade. The steamboats would disappear within 50 years due to the nationwide network of railroads. Lincoln had a hand in that, too, as we will see.

In partnership with his good friend Bill Herndon, he handled a variety of cases large and small, from property rights of individual citizens and the railroads to personal injury, damage suits, horsethievery and murder. Lincoln "came to know in whispered consultation and public cross-examination the minds and hearts of a quarreling, chaffering, suspicious, murdeous, loving, lavish, paradoxical humanity" (p. 406). He was actively involved in "the philosophy of changing civilizations and technical engineering as well as the economic structure of the society in which he was living" (p. 391).

Just as physicians have (or should have) a "bedside manner," attorneys have a "courtroom manner." Lawyer Lincoln was a blend of **surgeon** and **ole philosopher** with a dash of **ole yeller** from time to time for flavor. He was tall, thin and awkward in appearance with hard lines in his gaunt face and quite frequently a look of melancholy in his eyes. Quiet, unassuming, modest and self-deprecating, he would sometimes sit in court whittling on a piece of wood with a pocket knife, laid back with his feet on the table. His appearance and manner was sometimes misperceived by his courtroom adversaries who underestimated him, to their later shock and undoing. Beneath his gracious country-boy behaviors there was much intelligence, knowledge skill, common sense and wisdom. He could be actively alert and direct or warm, accepting and caring. The following cases and stories chronicle the attitude and behaviors of this "prairie lawyer."

An "old farmer" bought a flock of sheep one summer on consignment with a signed agreement to pay for them in the spring when, fattened by feeding on his crops, he could pay for them with the money they would fetch. He worked hard, tending them and feeding them all through the winter. Tragically, they all died in the spring. The sheep owner sued for his money. The old farmer couldn't pay. Lincoln defended him. "The first trial was a mistrial; the second trial was lost and the cost and damages stripped the old man of nearly all his property. At seventy he was starting west to hunt cheap land and make a new home. As he shook hands with the old man and said good-bye, Lincoln's eyes were wet and he had to hold back tears" (p. 392).

A widow of a Revolutionary War soldier hired Lincoln to represent her in a claim to recover half of a $400 pension taken as fee by a pension agent. His partner "Billy" Herndon recalled Lincoln's testimony after he "put the tottering widow on the witness stand where she told her story through her tears":

> She was not always thus. She was once a beautiful young woman. Her step was elastic, her face as fair, and her voice as sweet as any that rang in the mountains of old Virginia. But now she is poor and defenseless. Out here on the prairies of Illinois, many hundreds of miles from the scenes of her childhood she appealed to us who enjoy the privileges achieved for us by the patriots of the Revolution, for our

> sympathetic aid and manly protection. All I ask is, shall we befriend her? (p. 403)

He then painted a vivid verbal picture of the suffering of the Revolutionary War soldiers. Herndon observed that "some of the jurymen wept." Lincoln won the case, but he was not finished. He paid the widow's hotel bill, her railroad ticket back home, and he mailed her the check for the full amount of the pension. He did not charge any fee for his services.

Lincoln's caring while genuine, had practical advantages. Choosing jurors in a murder case in which he represented the defendant, he "tried to find some ground of old acquaintance." "Your name?" he asked one. "William Killian." "Bill Killian. Tell me, are you the son of old Jake Killian?" "Yes sir." "Well, you are a smart boy if you take after your dad" (p. 398).

His anger could be as powerful an emotion as his kindness. While representing the defendant in a murder trial, the judge overruled him several times. During a recess, Lincoln told his partner Herndon he was "determined to crowd the court to the wall." When the trial was resumed, Herndon observed that he "gradually got the judge puzzled and lost" by reciting "authorities to show that the great jurists and the lessons of the past were against the judge." He continued relentlessly and "hurled facts and questions fast from point to point . . . was contemptuous of the court in manner, voice, insinuation and allegation, without being technically guilty of contempt of court." Herndon concluded that it was "a superb performance . . . he peeled the court from head to foot . . . the judge reversed his decision in Lincoln's favor . . . I shall never forget the scene" (p. 403).

The conventional stereotype of "honest Abe" in his teens and early adulthood is confirmed in his "prairie years" while a practicing attorney. A woman hired him to have her land surveyed and he did so, discovering that the old deed was in error. Three acres were really the property of the heirs of a neighbor. He wrote a letter to her advising her to pay the market price for the three acres. She declined. He wrote a second letter, informing her "the Matheny heirs were poor and needed the money." She was unmoved. He wrote a third letter, restating his position and explaining to her that what he was asking "seemed to him plain justice. She sent him payment in full and he hunted up the heirs and shared them out the money" (p. 392).

Lincoln himself was on the receiving end of a client who refused to pay him. The Illinois Central Railroad was exempted by the state legislature from paying taxes for its right of way. In 1853, McLean County assessed and billed the railroad. The cost would "mount into millions and bankrupt the corporation." Lincoln represented the railroad. He lost in circuit court and appealed to the state supreme court and won a reversal of the lower court's decision. He submitted his bill for $2,000. He was paid $200. He filed suit against the railroad for $5,000 and won a judgment in that amount. But the railroad did not pay and after waiting two months "an executive order was issued directing the sheriff to seize property of the railroad." The fee was paid (pp. 382-383).

In another case, an opposing attorney said to the jury: "You have been listening for the last hour to an actor who knows well how to play the role of seeming, for effect." Lincoln "doubled out of the chair [and] solemn, cool, wrathy and eying the other lawyer said, "You have known me for years and you know that not a word of that language can be truthfully applied to me." The opposing attorney immediately retracted his statement, saying, "I take it all back, Mr. Lincoln" (p. 402).

He would interrupt co-counsel on his own side to prevent what he perceived to be unfair or improper. When Amzi Williams, handling a witness on Lincoln's side of a case, called out, "Oh! No! No! No!" Lincoln stood with a slow yelling of "Oh! Yes! Yes! Yes!" putting a stop to the bulldozing of the witness (p. 402).

Abraham Lincoln did his homework. He researched his cases well. In an 1857 murder case, an eyewitness testified he saw a fight between the defendant and the victim "between ten and eleven o'clock at night and by the light of the moon shining nearly straight over them." Lincoln "sent out for an almanac" and showed that the moon set at 11:57 P.M. that night. Not only was it impossible to be "nearly straight over" anyone, but there would not be enough light to see clearly (pp. 398-399).

On May 6, 1856, the steamboat **Annie Afton** rammed into pilings of the Rock Island Railroad bridge across the Mississippi River. In view of the great animosity between the railroads and the steamer companies, it was very probably an "intentional accident." The ship and the bridge caught fire. "Steamboaters up and down the Mississippi had a jubilee . . . ringing of bells and blowing of whistles on all boats in view of the burning, sagging truss of the bridge." The boat owners sued for damages! Lincoln represented the railroad. Engineers, pilots, boat owners, river men and bridge builders were called as witnesses.

Lincoln studied background information so well that there was laughter when he would correct a witness on a matter of feet or inches or the span of a truss. Sitting whittling and seemingly lost to the world, he suddenly sprang to his feet, demanded the original notes as to certain measurements and the testifying expert witness was shown to be mistaken; it has its effect on the jury. He analyzed the angles of piers, the curve of the river, the depth of the channel, the velocity of the current and showed the final smash of the boat was in the splash door aft of the wheel. He proved the ship's captain ran his boat as though the river had no bridge with piers standing in it.

In his final statement suming up the case "the main drive" of his argument was that one man had as good a right to cross a river as another had to sail up or down it. He pointed out the "growing travel from east to west that had to be considered; it was as important as the Mississippi traffic. It was growing larger and larger, this east-to-west traffic, building up new country with a rapidity never before seen in the history of the world . . . this current of travel has its rights as well as that of north and south." Mindful of the time, he concluded with: "Gentlemen, I have not exhausted my stock of information and there are more things I could suggest regarding this case, but as I have doubtless used up my time I presume I had better close." The jury retired and "when they came out they had agreed to disagree; their action was generally taken as a victory for railroads, bridges and Chicago as against steamboats, rivers and St. Louis" (pp. 386-387).

Abraham Lincoln was a conscientious advocate for his clients, a worthy adversary to his opponents and a credit to the legal profession. He exemplified Wendell Phillips Stafford's prescription that "the ideal lawyer must be adequately endowed by nature, fully informed by study, perfectly disciplined by practice, open-eyed to his opportunity and loyal to his trust" (**The lawyer**). He satisified, too, the observation of our old friend Cicero (106-43 B.C.) that "the aim of forensic oratory is to teach, to decide, to move" (**De Optimo, Genere Oratoriumn**). Lincoln's commitment to the adversary system to test the truth of both sides is reflected in his comment that "there are few things wholly evil or wholly good; almost everything is an inseparable compound of the two" (p. 405).

When he had become better known, toward the end of his "prairie years," a group of citizens approached him and asked him to draw up the papers incorporating a town in Logan County which would be the county seat. He asked them what the new town should be called and they told him "to name it Lincoln." He reflected a moment, smiled broadly and said: "You better not do that, for I never knew anything named Lincoln that amounted to much" (p. 391). He was, to the end of his life, a man of great compassion and great humility. He was a loving man, a lovely man—and he was a lawyer.

REFERENCES

Braude, J. M. (Ed.) (1984). *Braude's treasury of wit and humor.* Englewood Cliffs, NJ: Prentice-Hall.

Buescher, W. M. (Ed.) (1984). *Walt Buescher's library of humor.* Englewood Cliffs, NJ: Prentice-Hall.

Curiae, A. (Ed.) (1947). *Law in action: An anthology of law in literature.* New York: Bonanza Books.

Benet, S. V. (1947). The devil and Daniel Webster. In A. Curiae (Ed.), *Law in action: An anthology of law in literature.* New York: Bonanza Books.

Dershowitz, A. M. (1982). *The best defense.* New York: Random House.

France, A. (1947). Crainquebille. In A. Curiae (Ed.), *Law in action: An anthology of law in literature.* New York: Bonanza Books.

Keeton, R. E. (1973). *Trial, tactics and methods.* Second edition. Boston: Little, Brown.

Kester, J. G. (1987). Too many lawyers? *Reader's Digest,* April, 1987, 153-160.

Kurke, M. I., & Meyer, R. G. (Eds.) (1986). *Psychology in product liability and personal injury litigation.* Washington, DC: Hemisphere Publishing.

MacHovec, F. J. (1984). *Courtroom survival.* Danville, VA: Author.

Sandburg, C. (1936). *The people, yes.* New York: Harcourt, Brace.

Sandburg, C. (1947). Prairie lawyer. In A. Curiae (Ed.), *Law in action: An anthology of law in literature.* New York: Bonanza Books.

Sullivan, T. (1986). Putting professionalism back into lawyering. *Richmond Times-Dispatch,* Friday, November 28, 1986, page A-13.

CHAPTER 5

EXPERT WITNESS PRACTICE DETAILS

Law logic, an artificial system of reasoning exclusively used in courts of justice but good for nothing anywhere else.

John Quincy Adams
(1767-1848)

EXPERT WITNESSES provide courts, judges and juries with specialized information they need to understand a case which is not otherwise available to them. Expert witnesses analyze facts, educate the court on how a science, profession or trade approaches a real or hypothetical situation, and give a considered opinion on it. Once you are qualified by the court, there is the legal duty to "tell the truth, the whole truth and nothing but the truth" binding on all witnesses but also the ethical and moral obligation to remain objective and "tell it like it is" to the best of your ability, according to the current "state of the art" in your field. Cicero (106-43 B.C.) included these priorities in his admonition to historians: "The first law is never to dare utter an untruth. The second is to suppress nothing that is true. Moreover, there should be no partiality or malice . . . " (**De Oratore, II, 62**).

In court while testifying, attorneys on both sides will strive to use an expert's testimony to further their case. That is their sworn duty and in some cases they pursue this goal with a seemingly "end-justifies-the-means" attitude that can cut into the witness's self-confidence and self-esteem. Regardless of verbal and non-verbal approaches of opposing attorneys, the expert witness should carefully consider whatever is written and stated to ensure that it reflects the truth and follows Cicero's admonition. In "the heat of battle," by making no overstatement in contested cases when your testimony is pivotal, it is difficult to retain composure and self-confidence, much like holding a ship on course in a severe storm.

HIRED GUN V. VILLAGE BLACKSMITH

In the mental health field, there are now diplomates in forensic psychiatry and psychology who undergo postgraduate written and oral examinations on law and courtroom procedures. They are expert witness specialists—"professional witnesses." It is not unusual to have such highly credentialled professionals on both sides of a case, their testimony diametrically opposed. "Hired gun" or, an even less delicate term, "whore" are sometimes used to describe "professional witnesses" whose major livelihood is testifying in court. The implication is that they will sell their opinion if the price is right. Experts on the prosecution side in criminal cases have been called "hangmen" or "executioners." These are derogatory terms, **ad hominem** attacks, humiliating and reprehensible, but the more frequently an expert testifies the more likely someone will use them. "It comes with the territory."

While highly credentialled expert witnesses have the most impressive qualifications in terms of education, training and experience, there are some attorneys who do not use them, preferring instead educated, knowledgeable, experienced practitioners or highly skilled workers in the field relevant to the case. "A full-time practitioner," Ostroff writes, "will have more knowledge, skill and experience about his field than someone who spends much of his time in court" and "may have more training and education" (1982, p. 8). "Training" and "education" are those terms used in **Federal Rule 702.** Ostroff contends professional witnesses are "less credible . . . ready to render any helpful opinion so long as the pay is right," but a "full-time practitioner is not as subject to this criticism." As they devote more and more time to court work and less to full-time work or practice, professional witnesses must rely more on books, articles, research and the work of others rather than actual "hands-on" daily experience. An expert is more convincing if testimony is based on firsthand knowledge and experience: "The full-time practitioner who does every day what he is testifying about is more likely to be believed than one who testifies every day about what he seldom does" (p. 8).

"Hired guns" have an advantage similar to the gunfighters in the days of the Wild West. They're good at what they do. Generally, they're prepared for all the varieties of courtroom "gunfights" because of their experience in many courts. Ostroff agrees: "Professional witnesses do have one advantage: often, they are more adept at communicating their knowledge to the jury." This is especially effective when testimony involves complex, technical subjects. Momjian (1983) agrees: "The simple fact that the witness has past court experience makes his testimony more convincing" and adds that if the expert has had actual experience "in similar situations, testimony is likely to be better received" (p. 10). "Despite this advantage," Ostroff advises, "you should generally avoid them." He prefers the hardworking "village blacksmith" who labors daily at the anvil. For those with limited courtroom experience called upon to testify as an expert witness, Ostroff's observations should help bolster self-confidence.

SELECTING EXPERT WITNESSES

It is the attorney's responsibility to search for competent, credible experts appropriate to the case. There are court-appointed experts in certain selected cases such as in divorce proceedings to appraise or divide property (Krafte, 1982). Both defense and plaintiff must accept the court-appointed expert. The vast majority of cases in which expert witnesses are used involve selection by lawyers on both sides.

Momjian (1983) feels "the best expert is one whose substantive positive is consistent with your client's case but who has other qualities that give a certain 'glow' to an otherwise acceptable position. In fact, the best expert testimony in the world may be utterly useless unless it is presented by someone whose other attributes can add a ring of truth to it" (p. 8). In other words, it is not so much what you say as how you say it, or better stated for purposes of this book, it is as much how you say it as what you say. It is "stage presence," a blend of fact and certainty, of honesty and sincerity and enthusiasm, competence and credibility, truth and timing.

Inker (1983) recommends that attorneys choose an expert whose unique skill, knowledge or experience is relevant to evidentiary needs and is "beyond the common knowledge or understanding of the fact-finder" (p. 11). Daniels (1984) prefers an expert who can be "a colleague while at the same time preserving objectivity" (p. 66). Usually, the attorney-expert initial contact is a mutual "feeling for a fit" between legal needs unique to the case and the expert's area of competence. More experienced and more perceptive lawyers and experts "get a feel" for each other at this time as well as a "fix" on what kind of data and analysis is needed for the case.

COMPARATIVE CREDIBILITY

Imagine two experts testifying, the first a person 25 yeas old, slouching in the chair, wearing casual clothing, worn blue jeans, eyes cast downward, talking to the floor. The second expert is a person over 50, sitting upright and alert, with good eye contact with judge, jury and lawyers, wearing tasteful, conservative clothing. The first expert is a high school or college graduate, the second is a licensed "doctor" (Ph.D. or M.D.), author of a book and several professional journal articles and who has addressed state, national and international conferences. Their testimony can be identical, but the second expert is likely to be more credible, more convincing. **What** each says is equally **admissible,** but the second expert's testimony will have more impact, in legal terms more **weight,** because of a combination of positive factors. Attorneys search for the ideal expert witness, a person with as many of the following "virtues" (my term) or "plus" factors as possible:

12 VIRTUES OF AN IDEAL EXPERT WITNESS

1. Education and/or Training. Many lawyers believe "educational background and training of the expert are the most important criteria in qualifying a witness" (Momjian, 1983, p. 8). For professional persons, "plus" factor are undergraduate and graduate degrees, perferably from prestigious schools, academic honors if any, and postgraduate education, courses, workshops and certificate programs. Technical, skilled experts can refer to tradeschools, apprenticeships, certificates, and especially courses taken by recognized authorities. For all expert witnesses, it is important to list dates of education and training and the length of time involved. A 40-hour certificate program based on an examination is more impressive than a one-day seminar.

2. Current and previous employment and positions in business or a profession and their status, involving a high level of expertise, number and type of employees supervised, scope and depth of skills needed. Positions should ideally reflect increasing skill, responsibility and leadership. Full-time work in any field carries more weight than part-time work. Government service suggests credibility: "The public believes that people who serve governmental units or organizations are more credible than those who do not" (Momjian, 1983, p. 10).

3. Years of experience, in one's occupation and profession but also augmented by practical, relevant life experience. A well-credentialled marriage counselor scores high on education but if married five times loses some credibility. A child custody expert is more credible if s/he is also a parent. Looking "too young" implies lack of knowledge, skills and experience; it does not appear you can be "too old," since age in court generally adds to credibility. There are cases where the personal, physical traits of a witness can add to credibility, such as sex (female witness for a rape victim), race (cases involving racial discrimination), national origin (immigration), even military service (Vietnam veterans and post-traumatic stress disorder).

4. Court Experience. Plus factors are: out-of-state testimony; variety of types of courts "makes testimony more convincing" (Momjian, 1983, p. 10); and number of similar cases. Negative factors: always testifying on the same side (defendant or plaintiff; husband or wife; men or women) or for the same lawyer or firm; and no previous court experience or similar cases.

5. Licenses and/or certificates, especially where there are strict requirements, state or federal regulations. Dates and years of licensure are plus factors. An FAA-licensed instructor or commercial airline pilot with 20 years' experience would be more credible than a private pilot with two years' experience in cases relevant to aviation, all else being equal. Generally, the more years of experience add to witness credibility.

6. Publications and Citations. Books and articles authored by the expert and referred to or quoted by others are plus factors, demonstrating that the expert's work (and opinion) is a useful resource and reference for others in the field.

7. Teaching and Presentations. "Triers of fact have greater respect for an expert who teaches others than an expert who has no such qualifications . . . the longer the teaching experience the more qualified the expert appears" (Momjian, 1983, p. 10). Undergraduate and graduate credit courses, advanced seminars and postgraduate continuing education for professional experts and similar training activities for technical-industrial experts increase credibility. Titles such as Visiting, Assistant,

Associate or Full Professor augment the positive effect of the expert's testimony. Speeches, workshops, seminars, panels and the like at state, regional, national and international meetings add further to the expert's impact.

8. Consulting. Being consulted, informally or formally, preferably by title (such as printed on business cards, stationery and phone book yellow pages listings and in correspondence of others) for individuals and firms and serving on key task forces, committees, commissions or special projects distinguishes the expert witness as a respected authority. This impression is intensified the more prestigious the organization receiving the consultation (Fortune 500 corporations; major state and federal agencies). Serving on key task forces, committees, commissions, community and/or service boards or on special projects further enhances an expert's stature and persuasive influence.

9. Relevant Memberships Leadership Roles. Appointive and elective offices in professional or technical organizations, associations and societies are plus factors. Experts in child custody cases who are members of family therapy and divorce-mediation organizations will have more weight than the same testimony by experts without such memberships, all else being equal (education, training, license and years of experience).

10. Honors, Awards, Distinctions. Special awards and honors, patents and inventions, innovations acknowledge as making a unique contribution in fields relevant to the case on trial, are all plus factors contributing to greater credibility.

11. Physical Traits: Appearance and Mannerisms. Older witnesses are more credible than younger experts. Those who sit upright, head up and speak clearly and confidently give the impression they know what they're talking about. Inker (1983) urged attorneys "also consider the manner and style in which the expert responds. Answers should be direct and plainly stated." Expert witnesses should not respond as if "merely reading aloud from a curriculum vitae. Conveying information in a meaningful way is as essential as the contents" (p. 11).

12. Mental/Psychological Traits: Interested and Committed. Expert witnesses are more effective who share with judges and attorneys belief in the basic principles and ideals of law (Chap. 2), who give time and effort to a case and not just expertise, and who have testified in other cases to the satisfaction of both judges and attorneys.

When an attorney presents an expert witness to the court to be qualified, the "virtues" are emphasized and qualifications the expert does not have are omitted. The expert is presented in his or her best light. There are some exceptions to this. In many jurisdictions a medical doctor's opinion has more weight than that of nonmedical experts. The opinion of a family medical practitioner with very little psychiatric training, based on a 15-minute interview immediately before trial, was given more weight than that of a clinical psychologist based on several hours of tests and twenty hours of observation of the defendant in psychotherapy. In that jurisdiction, medical doctors without psychiatric specialization could commit patients to mental hospitals for psychiatric examination. Psychologists did not have this privilege. Medical doctors had higher status (legally and in the public eye) and thus higher credibility.

A 60-year-old deputy sheriff with 40 years' experience in full-time law enforcement may be less credible than a much younger Ph.D. from the FBI Academy. But an "old philosopher" attorney might "turn the tables" on the bright young expert by emphasizing the old sheriff's wisdom, judgment and experience. A skilled attorney can effect a profound change in the courtroom climate to enhance or reduce witness credibility. Expert witness virtues, in and of themselves, are always relative to the witness, to other witnesses, and to the informational needs unique to the case. Also, they are always in dynamic balance with the external realities in the community, applicable case law and local legal practice.

EXPERT WITNESS CREDIBILITY CHECKLIST

(Experts can score themselves and attorneys can evaluate and compare potential witnesses, using the following ten factors. Score each factor on the scale shown, then add up all entries. A "perfect" witness with maximum points on all factors would score 100.)

FACTOR	SCORE (0-10)
1. Education and/or training (M.D. or Ph.D. = 10)	
2. Years of relevant experience (1 point = 2 years, maximum 5; point each court case as expert witness, maximum 5)	
3. Current/previous relevant employment (3 + positions with increasing responsibility = 10)	
4. Licenses/certificates (with rigorous regs/laws = 10)	

5. Consulting experience
   (1 point for each year and firm or
   person consulted: maximum 10)
6. Publications/citations
   (book or several articles = 5;
   cited in works of others = 5)
7. Teaching/presentations
   (1 point each course/workshop: max 5;
   1 point each state, national, or
   international presentation: max 5)
8. Relevant memberships/leadership
   (1 point each organization: max 5;
   1 point for each appointive or
   elective office held: max 5)
9. Honors/awards/dictinctions
   (1 point for each, maximum 10)
10. Personal factors
   (Appearance, manner: max 5;
   interest, commitment: max 5)

X. (Extra unscored question)
   Fees fair and reasonable? _____ Yes _____ No

QUALIFYING AN EXPERT WITNESS

Though it is the judge who actually **qualifies** expert witnesses, attorneys select them and it is their responsibility to present them to the court. This is much more than a mere procedural step. The presentation itself—how it is done—can lend support to and reinforce the attorney's case before the expert even gives an opinion. "The qualification process serves a dual purpose," Inker maintains, because "it lays a foundation for the admissibility of the expert's opinion and enhances the credibility of that testimony" (1983, p. 11). He recommends that attorneys "present qualifications in a way that makes an effective initial impact. If credibility is enhanced from the outset, a favorable impression is more likely to be sustained" (ibid.). Daniels (1984) held that "experts play a significant and sometimes decisive role in modern litigation" and an attorney's "major task is to minimize the intrusion of your adversary's discovery" and "spare the expert witness from having to deal with unnecessarily difficult cross-examination" (p. 64).

Inker emphasizes verbal and nonverbal skills to help attorneys gain and hold judge or jury interest and maximize the impact of expert witness qualifications: "You, in asking the questions, are as responsible for the presentation as the expert who is responding. By the inflection of your voice, try to make the expert's testimony in qualification come alive. If you lose the interest of the trier of fact at the qualification stage, you might just as well save the expert's testimony for another day" (ibid.).

TYPICAL QUALIFYING QUESTIONS

Attorneys will ask questions in the qualification process which demonstrate the witness' competence and expertise in the area relevant to the case and the needs of the court for information. The following is an example of questions an attorney would ask an accountant testifying as an expert witness for a physician's wife in a divorce case. They are adapted from Albert Momjian's 1983 article in **The Family Advocate** (p. 44):

1. State your name and your business address.
2. What is your occupation?
3. State your education, including college and graduate school.
4. How many years have you been an accountant?
5. Is accounting your full-time profession?
6. Are you a certified public accountant?
7. What are the requirements to a certified public accountant?
8. Do you have others working for you? How many are accountants? How many others?
9. Describe briefly your accounting experience with respect to services provided to individuals, firms and organizations.
10. Describe accounting services you have provided to physicians.
11. What type of medical practices or specialization did these physicians have?
12. Do you belong to any accounting organizations or associations? If so, what are they?
13. Have you written any books or articles in the accounting field? If so, what are they?
14. Do you have any teaching experience? If so, briefly describe it.
15. Have you testified in court before? If so, in what types of cases and how many times?
16. Was your previous testimony at the request of attorneys other than me?
17. Have you testified for governmental agencies? If so, briefly describe that experience.

18. Have you testified as an expert accountant in other divorce proceedings? If so, state whether you testified only for husbands, for wives or both.
19. Have you testified in cases similar to this one? If so, how many times and in which courts?
20. Do you have any personal, social or business relationship with either of the parties to this litigation?

Of course, attorneys should avoid questions which will not be answered affirmatively or where the expert does not have clearly demonstrable experience. If there are opposing experts, questions should be asked which imply greater competence and prestige for the attorney's witness.

Since attorneys must report to the court witnesses they expect to use, opposing attorneys will have this information beforehand. They will have the opportunity to research a witness' background, perhaps "dig up some dirt" to use to disqualify the witness from testifying. If opposing experts have a long list of impressive credentials, most attorneys will **stipulate** those qualifications. This means there is then no need to ask questions such as those shown above. In this way the judge and jury do not learn the extensive expertise of the witness: "If your expert's qualifications are far outweighed by those of the other side's, **qualification by stipulation** or by written documentation might prove advantageous. But if your expert has credentials far superior to those of your opponent's, these methods may hurt your case" (Momjian, 1983, p. 44).

Another tactic to impose controls on experts is to have them **sequestered,** excluded from the courtroom in a "witness room" or some other room adjoining the courtroom or nearby. Most attorneys don't like to have opposing witnesses sitting in court listening to all the testimony before being sworn in and giving their own testimony. They justifiably fear that testimony can be influenced by the development of the case. And it's a lot easier to interrogate an opposing witness if s/he has no idea what has happened before they step inside the courtroom.

WHAT'S DISCOVERABLE?

Discovery is the pretrial process of obtaining as much information as possible from the opposing side. **Federal Rules 26-37** provide for the scope and the procedures for pretrial discovery and "protection from overreaching." Most states have followed the lead of the federal rules which describe five discovery devices: interrogatories, depositions, requests for document (or other materials) inspection, physical or mental examinations, and requests for admission (McCoid, 1974, p. 263).

There are two kinds of privileged information excluded or immune from the discovery process in most jurisdictions. They are **privilege by content** which includes military, commercial, trade or state secrets, and 5th amendment protection against self-incrimination and **privilege by context,** the confidential relationships of physician-patient or attorney-client. These can be overcome by disclosure **in camera** (in the judge's private chamber or office) provided the holder of the privilege agrees. Immunity can also be overcome if it can be proved to the court there is "substantial need to know," an inability to get the information elsewhere or if getting it elsewhere constitutes "undue hardship."

INTERROGATORIES

Interrogatories are written questions submitted to you by the opposing attorney usually answered in writing under oath within a stated time limit. The object is to obtain the substance of your testimony and the basis of your opinion. Not all cases will require interrogatories. **Federal Rule 26(c)** protects the party receiving interrogatories from embarrassment, annoyance, oppression, or undue burden or expense. Privileged information by content or context is immune, though as has been noted above, it can be accessed under certain conditions.

Interrogatories identify witnesses, access the facts, sources, grounds and damages of the plaintiff and "fix" or "freeze" the plaintiff's case, because they limit the trial process to details contained within the total discovery process. There are some problems with interrogatories. Experts sometimes collaborate with attorneys in answering interrogatories, specifically what to answer, not how or how much. Responses are supposed to be the expert's, not the attorney's, and from a strictly ethical point of view any change in wording by a third party introduces bias. Interrogatories may not be clearly worded, or may be incomplete, or may miss some important details which limit or weaken the case for the side asking the questions. They are fixed as any written words are and in this sense rigid and inflexible. Questioners can't probe, elaborate or further develop information when limited only to an exchange of written material. The face-to-face interaction of deposition or the trial process do that far better.

DEPOSITIONS

Depositions are questions asked of **deponents** under oath by opposing attorneys before someone authorized to swear oaths, often the person recording. After the opposing attorney reviews answers to interrogatories, depositions may be requested to obtain further or additional background information. Depositions are frequently held in attorney's offices. They are used when a person with needed information is not available to testify in court. Litigating parties or nonlitigants (nonparties) can be asked to make depositions. Nonparties are usually subpoenaed; litigants are requested through counsel. Cross examination is appropriate at deposition hearings. Objections and questions as to admissibility of presented material or testimony are noted for disposition later in court—the person administering oaths has no authority to rule on objections. Failure to object at deposition waives the right to correct errors later in court. A deponent who refuses to answer a question can be forced to do so by court order. In such cases the deposition hearing is recessed while the attorney who requested deposition seeks the court order. McCoid (1974) reports that "oral deposition is the most widely used of all devices" (p. 266).

Critique

Interrogatories and depositions add to the cost of litigation and they can be inconvenient and time consuming. On the other hand, they can provide valuable information of the "cards held" by the other side, the factual basis of their case, who will testify and with what scope and depth. Attorneys can in these ways "feel out" the adversary, meet, observe and "size up" their expert witnesses, and "tease out" and probe the basis of their position. Careful study of questions asked in interrogatories and "tracking" the line of questioning at deposition hearings can expose the adversary's strategy to be used later in the trial process. Many cases are settled out of court on the basis of information developed in interrogatories and depositions.

Some attorneys "coach" their expert witnesses in how (not what) to respond to interrogatories and depositions. For example, it is **always** wise to pause a few moments before answering at deposition hearings to give "your" attorney time to object if there is a need to do so. Answering interrogatory questions simply and to the point, with minimal verbiage, gives the opposing attorney less material to use against you. Generally, expert witnesses should never volunteer information or overanswer questions, in interrogatories, at deposition hearings—or in court.

Unfortunately, some "yes" or "no" answers can be gross oversimplifications, "playing into the hands" of opposing counsel by enabling him or her to make conclusions later in court which are unwarranted by the facts. You should meet with the attorney requesting your testimony before deposition (but not before interrogatories) to discuss what kind of questions require more complete responses. Doing so does not in any way change your opinion but protects it from incursions and possible distortion by opposing counsel.

PRODUCTION FOR INSPECTION

Federal Rule 34 allows for requests for inspection of "tangibles," documents or other materials from parties in litigation. Such requests can be served to either litigant and designate the tangible to be inspected and the date, time, place and inspection method. They are often used in antitrust actions and less frequently in personal-injury cases. The party being served the request has two choices: (1) to submit or (2) "stall" by stating an objection. The requesting party can seek to overcome the objection by a court order requiring the inspection. McCoid (1974) reported that "production for inspection is a valuable and regularly used device, though it is not as popular as depositions or interrogatories" (p. 270).

PHYSICAL OR MENTAL EXAMINATION

Federal Rule 35 provides for physical or mental examinations or submission of previous such examinations of litigating parties or nonparties "for good cause." Examinations are used to confirm or deny extent of plaintiff's injuries, determine biological parentage in paternity suits, or as evidence a defendant could have or did cause or contribute to injury or damages. The examining professional is selected by the requesting party, but the opposing side can have its own examiner present or an expert witness later at trial proceedings to challenge findings.

REQUEST FOR ADMISSION

Federal Rule 36 provides for requests by one litigating party to another for admission specific to the "genuineness" of facts, applications of law to fact, and to documents. The challenging party can admit or deny knowledge of or information relative to genuineness. McCoid (1974) reported that while requests for admission "enlarge the scope of discovery" and have "great potential for simplifying proof and narrowing the issues that require trial," they are "little used" (p. 272). He estimated that about one in four litigants use them and less than half of them succeed.

Let's now examine standard legal practices involving expert witnesses for the standpoint of their discoverability.

INITIAL CONTACT WITH ATTORNEY

Whenever an attorney phones to ask if you are interested in testifying in a case, make a written note of the date, time, name and what was discussed. In certain circumstances you can be asked to describe every call from the attorney. This is a tactic to claim these contacts influenced your opinion and biased your judgment. Both you and the attorney should ask specific questions of each other to have a clear understanding of what is needed. How much of your time is likely to be needed? How will you be paid? Fees can be a flat rate, preferably paid in advance, hourly, or, in rare cases (and to be discouraged), a contingency. Travel to and from your office or home and room and board are expenses which should be included. It should be understood that you will be paid for your time while waiting to testify which can involve hours or days. In many cases, attorneys can arrange for expert testimony early in a case and thus "clear the decks for action" for their own adversarial courtroom combat.

Some experts are very sensitive to how questions are asked of them at this initial phase, resenting an attorney already advocating for one side. Ostroff (1982) suggests that his fellow attorneys ask only "whether or not certain facts and circumstances warrant a particular conclusion" and **not** "that a particular conclusion follows from certain facts and circumstances." I have never had any difficulty in this area. It is quite obvious from the phoned questions what the attorney is seeking. Experts can't possibly know in advance before any evaluation or research what their conclusions will be. To do so would of and by itself constitute bias, perhaps even fraud. If an expert's conclusions happen to coincide with the attorney's case, fine. If they do not, the attorney very likely will not choose to use that expert as a witness. If another expert's conclusion is supportive to the attorney's case, then that testimony will be used.

As eager and interested as you may be in a case, resist the temptation to discuss any more than the most general details until after your evaluation, examination, written report and interrogatories if any. You may be asked under oath in court to describe the date and time, scope and depth of the conversation, even what was said, in phone conversations and meetings with the attorney or any others involved in the case.

ENGAGEMENT LETTER

The next step usually is an **engagement letter** which confirms the expert's agreement to examine, evaluate, report and testify. The letter should clearly state pertinent questions, not answers. If there are legal concepts involved or subjects or areas to be explored, these should be stated but without any indication of the desired opinion. The letter should "avoid ambiguities, focus on the right questions, and emphasize the proper points . . . and diminish the possibility of confusion or misunderstanding and promote clarity in defining the expert's task" (Ostroff, 1982, p. 9). He adds an important word of caution to his fellow attorneys: "Draft it as though your opponent will read it."

SUBPOENA

To those who do not often testify as an expert witness, the subpoena process can be unsettling. A police car pulls up to the curb, a uniformed law enforcement officer, subpoena in hand, enters your office and asks for you. In a small town, that's enough to have tongues wagging for a three-block radius! Who **serves** the subpoena varies from state to state, but in most instances a federal marshal serves for federal courts and the sheriff for state courts, although "street clothed" process servers are also used. It's interesting how routine and unemotional this can become after testifying several times. I recall how apprehensive I felt when a uniformed officer, with gun and badge (he also wore sunglasses!), walked up to me, looked me in the eye and asked my name, handing me that official **writ** which **commanded** me to appear in court on the day and time specified.

There are two types of subpoena you are likely to receive: **subpoena ad testificandum** or a **subpoena duces tecum.** The first has always sounded to me like a prizewinning gourmet food and the second like a "deuces wild" poker hand. The **ad testificadum** type is an order to appear in court to testify at an investigation, trial or judicial proceeding. The **duces tecum** type is an order to appear in court but with the documents specified in the subpoena such as files, records, reports, books or papers. You should, therefore, read the subpoena to be certain you comply with it. In some jurisdictions, a subpoena can order an expert to make copies of documents and submit them to one of the attorneys in a case without the need for the expert to appear and testify. Grand juries and court clerks subpoena for trial, and state and federal government boards and commissions subpoena for hearings.

In most jurisdictions a subpoena includes name of the court, grand jury, board or commission, defendant and plaintiff names, case docket number, the courtroom, date and time you are to appear, any documents you must bring, the name and phone number of the attorney who got you into all this, the signature of the official issuing it, and any applicable witness fees. In some cases, experts get subpoenas to surrender records to the officer who served the subpoena which may violate confidentiality or privilege. A phone call to the court clerk and the attorney requesting your testimony will clarify whether or not you should submit the documents. Generally, the court clerk will ask the judge and any problems resolved. Failing to comply with a subpoena without just cause is a punishable offense, contempt of court.

COURT ORDER

A state or federal court, state or federal board or commission can issue a **court order.** Usually, they are issued to obtain certain documents and they have far more weight than a subpoena. It's easier to resist a subpoena than a court order. Refusing to comply with a court order is punishable with the charge of contempt of court, because doing so defies the court's authority. Court orders can be contested, revised and appealed but always through appropriate legal process. If you get a court order with which you in good conscience cannot comply, phone your attorney at once, while the court officer is there. If the attorney and no others are available, phone the court clerk or issuing authority.

SO WHAT'S DISCOVERABLE – REALLY?

Morgan Chu (1982) recommends to his fellow attorneys that the best rule is to assume "everything given or told to an expert witness may be discoverable" (p. 16). He bases his opinion on **Rule 26(b)(4)** of the **Federal Rules of Civil Procedure, Rules 612** and **705** of the **Federal Rules of Evidence,** and the U. S. Supreme Court "work product doctrine."

Rule 26, according to Chu, is an attempt to "untangle the mass of conflicting case law governing discovery from and about expert witnesses" (p. 13). Facts and opinions used in anticipation of litigation and trials are very definitely discoverable according to **Rule 26.** But some federal courts have ruled that "the mere possibility of future litigation" satisfies the **Rule 26** requirement of "anticipation of litigation or trial."

Discovery is achieved through interrogatories in which potential or intended witnesses are named together with the subject of their testimony and the basis of their opinions. But in **Pearl Brewing v. Schlitz Brewing, 415 F.Supp.1122 S.D.Tex. 1976** interrogatories were ruled unnecessary.

Expert consultant facts and opinions are discoverable "under exceptional circumstances," though some courts have denied such access (**Ager v. Stormont Hospital, 622 F.2d 496 (10th Cir.1980).** Still, consultant material is much less accessible than the facts and opinions of experts: "Broad discovery is available against the expert trial witness but the litigation consultant is largely immune" (Daniels, 1984, p. 64).

Rule 612 of the **Federal Rules of Evidence** holds that information an attorney gives to experts is discoverable. **Rule 705** makes discoverable information used by expert witnesses as the basis of their opinion in their direct examination testimony. Written affidavits and reports have "a legal life of their own" and experts should exercise great care in what is put in writing. In cross-examination, earlier drafts of documents are discoverable and the expert witness can be asked to explain every change from one version to the next. This inquiry can be integrated into phone calls and meetings between an attorney and the expert to suggest bias and subjectivity. Chu observes that "such cross-examination is at least embarrassing and it can be worse" (1982, p. 16). He recommends attorneys get an expert's opinion orally, write it themselves, then read it to the expert for approval and signature. If questioned in court, Chu maintains that it can be justified by the Supreme Court **work product doctrine,** that forcing disclosure of an expert witness's oral statements are not discoverable because they can reveal the attorney's "mental processes" (**Upjohn v. U.S., 449 U.S. 383, 399, 1981).**

In Hickman v. Taylor (1947), the U. S. Supreme Court opinion reflected the pro and con of the work product rule. Here are excerpts of that opinion as published in McCoid (1974, pp. 302 and 303):

> Here is simply an attempt without purported necessity or justification, to secure written statements, private memoranda and personal

> recollections prepared or formed by an adverse party's counsel in the course of his legal duties. As such, it falls outside the arena of discovery and contravenes the public policy underlying the orderly prosecution and defense of legal claims. Not even the most liberal of discovery theories can justify unwarranted inquiries into the files and the mental impressions of an attorney.
>
> Historically, a lawyer is an officer of the court and is bound to work for the advancement of justice while faithfully protecting the rightful interests of his clients. In performing his various duties, however, it is essential that a lawyer work with a certain degree of privacy, free from unnecessary intrusion by opposing parties and their counsel . . . .
>
> We do not mean to say that all written materials obtained or prepared by an adversary's counsel, with an eye toward litigation, are necessarily free from discovery in all cases. Where relevant and non-privileged facts remain hidden in an attorney's file and where production of those facts is essential to the preparation of one's case, discovery may properly be had.

In actual practice, discoverability varies from state to state, and state to federal courts. I have been asked at a deposition hearing to recall the date and time of initial contact with an attorney (it was a phone call), the length of the conversation and "exactly what was said." This suggests a conservative approach of limited contact between expert and attorney, orally and in writing. Some authorities recommend attorney-expert rehearsals of direct testimony, mock cross-examination and periodic review meetings "to modify, amplify or drop each project as circumstances and developments in the case may warrant" (Daniels, 1984, p. 67). But the same author cautions against "opening the door to otherwise unavailable lines of cross-examination" (p. 64).

As a practical matter, how best to proceed to minimize discoverability is a judgment call, a calculated risk best made by the attorney who is in a position to assess the pros and cons of how much contact is excessive and how much just enough. I recommend minimizing risk, a cautious awareness and conscious avoidance of anything that might "backfire," and minimal, brief contacts orally and in writing between attorneys and experts. My bias is that the only safe assumption is that everything you say and do may be discoverable. If it is, and your testimony is brief and to the point and attorney contacts likewise, there will be no loopholes. If it isn't, your testimony and contacts are concise and effective and you've lost nothing.

CONFLICTING TESTIMONY

Experts, given the same evidence in a case, can and do differ in their opinions. Not only does this bother many of the witnesses themselves, but it also can cause considerable public concern and controversy. The attempted assassination of President Reagan is an example of how a "contest of experts" on both sides confused and irritated the public who criticized the legal and justice systems. Experts can differ because they conduct their own study or examination, do their own research, and apply their own unique education and training, knowledge and skill to a specific case. While most experts agree to general principles, it is in the "nitty gritty," the finer points of specific cases, where differences arise due to the multiplicity of factors involved. Life **is** complex.

Confronting and processing differences, from the picayune to the profound, is a central principle and ideal of law. Such conflict provides the court with the raw materials from which truth is refined. Thomas Jefferson, in his First Inaugural Address on March 4, 1801, said that "error of opinion may be tolerated where reason is left free to combat it." Court is the verbal combat zone where opinion is weighted, the balance felt, and truth and fair judgment are realized. That's the ideal. Charles Evans Hughes (1862-1948), while Chief Justice of the U. S. Supreme Court, described the value of conflict and differences in a speech to the American Law Institute:

> How amazing it is that in the midst of controversies on every conceivable subject, one should expect unanimity of opinion upon different legal questions. In the highest ranges of thought, in theology, philosophy and science, we find differences of view on the part of the most distinguished experts . . . . The history of scholarship is a record of disagreements. And when we deal with questions relating to the principles of law and their applications, we do not suddenly rise into a stratosphere of icy certainty (Bartlett, 1968, p. 864).

TESTIMONY AS IDEA AND IDEAL

In their work, their product, both law and science seek to further refine truth. Courtwork, science and technology move by case and by experiment through successive approximations of truth. It has been so since the beginning of time, from stick to wheel to ball bearing to jet engine. St. Paul wrote almost 2,000 years ago "when that which is perfect is come then that which is imperfect shall be done away . for now we see through a glass, darkly, but then face to face" (Lamsa, 1933, p. 349). In 1841, Ralph Waldo Emerson reflected much the same idea: "Nature is a mutable cloud which is always and never the same" (Bartlett, 1968, p. 605). The ancient Buddhists taught that truth is like a diamond with many facets, each varying with light and the eye of the beholder. Mortimer Adler concluded that "defining truth is easy, knowing whether a particular statement is true is much harder; pursuing the truth the most difficult of all" (1972, p. 5).

KNOWLEDGE, OPINION, TRUTH

Adler (1972) differentiated knowledge from opinion: "It is knowledge when the object that we are thinking about compels us to think of it in a certain way. What we think then is not our personal opinion." If we are "free to make up our mind about it . . . then what we think is only an opinion" and "other rational persons can differ with us." By this test, much of what we "know" is actually opinion. Adler maintained that opinions "differ in their soundness." If based on "considerable evidence . . . while not conclusive" they are still "highly probable." If without "considerable evidence" they are nothing more than "wilful prejudices on our part" (p. 2).

Expert witnesses testify on product liability and personality dynamics, on practical realities and scientific phenomena. Some times the data is "hard," rooted in objective fact demonstrated by scientific or technological experiment and experience. Sometimes the data is "soft," the question asked, the testimony required, involving areas not yet definitively explored, or rigorously tested. In either application, the expert's own education, training, knowledge and skills form the basis for observation, analysis and conclusions, more than mere personal opinion. If there is personal opinion anywhere in the process, it will be challenged by the opposing attorney as hearsay. But how much of our contemporary arts and sciences, practices, trades, and technology are **knowledge** and how much is really **opinion**? Adler attempts to differentiate:

> This leaves open the question whether history, mathematics, experimental science and speculative philosophy should be classified as knowledge or opinion . . . . The extreme skeptic would say that they are all opinion though he might recognize that they have much more weight than mere personal opinions or private prejudices. The opposite view, which I would defend, is that we can have knowledge in the fields of mathematics and philosophy and highly probable opinion in the fields of experimental science and history (1972, p. 2).

Bartol (1983) describes four **ways of knowing** based on the work of the philosopher, Charles Pierce:

The first is the **method of tenacity** which is based on deep-seated long-held convictions and opinions "even in the face of contradictory evidence." Ethnic, racial and nationalistic prejudice fall into this category. The rationale is "as everyone knows" or "it's always been like that." These opinions can have some basis in fact, on earlier experience, custom (restrictive covenants), tradition (most nurses are women; most doctors are men) or history (age of consent). This is a historical method and is resistant to experimentation, external validation and change.

The **method of authority** is based on an external authority, some person, group or organization claiming to know the truth. The **learned treatise** tactic used to attempt to discredit an expert's testimony is an example of this method.

The **a priori method** (cause to effect) is a deductive method of reasonable assumptions, common sense or logical conclusions, from known previous causes applied to the present. **Legal precedents,** applying previous similar cases to current cases, is an example of this method.

The **method of science** is the empirical, experimental method shared by all the sciences. It is based on a specified definition, careful and objective observation, controlled testing under standard conditions and systematic, usually mathematical, analysis. It is an evolving, developing self-corrective process. Scientific journal articles are examples of this method. It is interesting to note that the heaviest weight of evidence, **beyond a reasonable doubt,** is based on more than 90 percent certainty, a lower test of proof than for science (.05 probability or 95 percent certainty).

Legal rules of evidence vary from a simple **preponderance** (more than 50-50 certainty) to the 90+ percent **beyond a reasonable doubt**, but amount, kind and source of evidence varies from case to case. Lawyer's choice of strategy will further vary the conditions under which "truth" is tested. Bartol (1983) points out that, unlike scientists, lawyers are free to "dabble in and out of the data pool and pick and choose" what to present, partial or complete, more or less relevant to the case (p. 18).

In a hotly contested court case, considerable time can be spent debating what is "true, most likely" or "most probable," as judged by evidence which is **relevant** and **material** in legal terminiology. The expert witness can be placed in a position of having to respond to questions at the cutting edge of what is known as differentiated from the unknown, the real from the potential, possible or probable, and asked to meticulously specify and definitively explain the difference. As we have seen in the words of Chief Justice Hughes, it is a most difficult distinction, even with respect to the law.

Monahan and Walkes (1985) contend that expert witness testimony based on scientific and objective knowledge should be considered legal fact, the highest status in law. This is a controversial and provocative subject, raising the question of how final, authoritative, definitive and universal an expert's considered opinion (or current science) can be. It is Adler's question asked again. And he got it from Socrates! Expert witnesses are in very good company.

Because THE truth is not always so easily seen despite the simple language of the oath "to tell the whole truth," judges, juries, attorneys and the public, through the sometimes selective or, worse, slanting of the media, can lose confidence in expert opinions. "A circus . . . zoo . . . tower of Babel" are some cynical characterizations I've heard from citizens about hotly contested cases where experts disagreed. The cynicism sometimes comes from philosophers and jurists as well. In his commencement address at Columbia University, the distinguished philosopher Nicholas Murray Butler (1862-1947) referred to an expert as "one who knows more and more about less and less." The late Jacob M. Braude, for 35 years a circuit court judge who heard hundreds of experts testify, described an expert as "one who has a good reason for guessing wrong." Elsewhere in his book he gave a more positive definition, friendlier to experts, and one I heartily recommend: "One who has all the answers if you ask the right questions" (Braude, 1964, p. 232).

Ideally, expert witnesses, examining the same data in a particular case, would arrive at the same conclusion. Socrates defined intelligence as knowing what you don't know. The more one knows about any given subject, the more exceptions, nuances and contradictions arise. Attorneys are quick to focus on exceptions, isolate and magnify them so that the exception is interpreted as the rule. It is a frequently used tactic and technique. To present a complex or technical subject to judge and jury in understandable language, concise yet comprehensive, is no simple task. Overanswer, overexplain, and you provide more material for opposing counsel to search for exceptions. Speak too briefly and you may deprive judge and jury of a clear understanding of facts and realities.

Experts should state opinions forthrightly, with confidence and conviction. In 1919, H. L. Mencken put it this way: "The public demands certainties and must be told definitely and a bit raucously that this is true and that is false" (Bartlett, 1968, p. 960). Always the realist and cynic, Mencken added: "But there are no certainties." Ostroff (1982) recommends that an expert's testimony "be organized like an assault on Mt. Everest: first, climb the mountain; second, plant a flag at the top; and third, climb down." The climb up is the "preparation, study, experimentation, rejection of alternative conclusions and analysis . . . to formulate conclusions or opinions." Stating an opinion, clearly and effectively, is "the flag at the pinnacle." The climb down is the expert explaining the basis of opinion.

Agreement among experts would be more easily attained outside the courtroom, without the restrictions imposed by the legal process. The **discovery process** controls what is included in the trial process; **the adversarial system,** by its nature, limits the scope and depth of testimony only to what is **legally** relevant and material between polar opposite positions with nothing (like the real nonlegal supralegal truth) in between. These factors greatly restrict a truly open, free search for truth. Law and the courts are a different world with different rules and practices than those of science and technology. The expert witness can only hope to remain true to her/his profession or occupation, give an opinion honestly and in good faith which is the purest truth or the best estimate of truth.

As we have seen, regardless of your opinion as an expert witness, you have a legal right and duty to place that opinion into testimony even if it differs markedly from others. It is only then that truth can shine through of its own light. The British political philosopher John Stuart Mill (1806-1873) explained why this process is so important as to be a sacred principle:

> The peculiar evil of silencing the expression of an opinion is that it is robbing the human race, posterity as well as the existing generation and those who dissent from the opinion still more than those who hold it. If the opinion is right, they are deprived of the opportunity of exchanging error for truth. If wrong, they lose what is almost as great as benefit, the clearer perception and livelier impression of truth produced by its collision with error . . . . We can never be sure that the opinion we are endeavoring to stifle is a false opinion, and if we were sure, stifling it would be an evil still . . . . Judgement is given to men that they may use it. Because it may be used erroneously, are men to be told they ought not to use it at all? (Webb, 1951, pp. 108-109).

USING A LAW LIBRARY

If you're going to spend a block of your time as an expert witness, you should learn how to use a law library. In some areas, these libraries are restricted to judges and lawyers, so it will be to your advantage to develop a consultative relationship with local attorneys who have requested your services as an expert consultant or witness.

Like any library, there is a definite method of arranging, filing and indexing material and a variety of sources containing state and federal case material from initial proceeding to appeal. A listing of a case is called a citation. The name which begins it is that of the plaintiffs, the party bringing suit, making the claim or preferring charges. In the fictitious case of **Cain v. Abel,** Cain is suing Abel. If Cain won and Abel then appealed, the appeals case (a new and separate proceeding at a state or appelate court) would be identified "cited" as **Abel v. Cain.** If there were criminal proceedings against Abel by the state, that criminal court case would be cited as **State v. Abel.** If there were federal charges, the citation would be **United States v. Abel.** There are numerals included in citations to help find them in the legal literature, as we will soon see.

Every state publishes its own **state reports,** a compendium of cases heard in that state. For example, **People v. Cole 382 Mich. 695 (1969)** refers you to the Michigan state reporter for 1969, volume 382 and to page 695. There is also a **regional reporter** for each of the regions of the country and a typical listing there is **Pierce v. Georgia, 254 S. E. 2d 838 (Georgia Supreme Court 1979),** referring to the 1979 regional reporter for the Southeastern United States for the designated case heard in the Georgia Supreme Court. The **American Digest System** divides cases into seven major categories, each with subsections of specific subjects. This takes a little getting used to, but it's not that difficult. The value of this publication is that it lists and cross-indexes every point of law involved in a case. The **Federal Supplement** lists cases heard in federal district courts, the **Federal Register** contains federal appeals court cases, **U. S. Reports** lists cases of the United States Supreme Court and the **Supreme Court Register** publishes summaries of United States Supreme Court proceedings. Federal cases are identified in the same way as state cases: **Bolton v. Harris, 395 F.2d 642 (D.C. Circuit 1968),** meaning Bolton sued Harris in federal court, second district in 1968 and the case can be found in volume 395, page 642. State and federal reporters and case digests usually have an index in the back to help you find the cases include in each volume.

In addition to these printed materials, there is now nationwide computer access by phone lines to law and case material data bases by several firms. Larger law firms as well as law libraries have this "computer connection" as well as subscriptions to the state and federal publications listed above and to helpful law journals, newsletters and magazines—more reason to make friends and colleagues of local attorneys. Law librarians are also a valuable resource. Like librarians in other settings, law librarians are helpful and cooperative. If you don't know where to look for needed information, ask them.

REFERENCES

Adler, M J. (1972). *Great ideas from the great books.* New York: Pocket Books.

American Bar Association (1983). For hire: Expert witness boom time. *American Bar Association Journal,* 69, 429-430.

Bartlett, J. (Ed.) (1968). *Familiar quotations: A collection of passages, phrases and proverbs traced to their sources in ancient and modern literature.* Boston: Little, Brown.

Bartol, C. R. (1983). *Psychology and American law.* Belmont, California: Wadsworth.

Braude, J. M. (Ed.) (1964). *Braude's treasury of wit and humor.* Englewood Cliffs, NJ: Prentice-Hall.

Chu, M. (1982). Discovery of experts. *Litigation,* 8, 13-16, 64.

Daniels, J. E. (1984). Managing litigation experts. *American Bar Association Journal,* 70, 64-67.

Inker, M. L. (1983). Make your testimony come alive. *Family Advocate,* 6, 11.

Krafte, C. W. (1982). How one judge cut the costs of expert witnesses. *Family Advocate,* 4, 13-15.

Lamsa, G. M. (1933). *The New Testament according to the Eastern Text.* Philadelphia, PA: Holman.

McCoid, J. C. (1974). *Civil procedure: Cases and materials.* St. Paul, MN: West.

Momjian, A. (1983). Preserving your witness's stellar testimony: How to qualify your expert to the court. *Family Advocate,* 6, 8-11 and 44.

Monahan, J., and Walkes (1985). Social authority: Obtaining, evaluating and establishing social science in law. *University of Pennsylvania Law Review,* 134, 477.

Morrill, A. E. (1972). *Trial diplomacy.* Second edition. Chicago, IL: Court Practice Institute.

Ostroff, P. I. (1982). Experts: A few fundamentals. *Litigation,* 8, 8-9 and 64.

Webb, K. B. (Ed.) (1951). *A source book of opinion on human values.* London, England: Tower Bridge.

CHAPTER 6

COPING AND SURVIVAL

Life is too short to waste
In critic peep or cynic bark,
Quarrel or reprimand;
'Twill soon be dark;
Up! Mind thine own aim
And God speed the mark!

Ralph Waldo Emerson
Poems (1847)

AS WE HAVE SEEN in previous chapters, law is both an ideal and a practical reality. One can indulge either—natural law as an extension of the laws of the universe or its Creator, or law as an amoral utilitarian means to an end, to the point where the end justifies any means. There is ample evidence of both in state and federal courts coast to coast. It may be that every case involves both sides of these philosophical polarities just as every case demonstrates the adversary system between defense and plaintiff.

To be solely an idealist would lessen your effectiveness as an expert witness. Court is another world, always a win-lose, black-and-white situation aimed at affecting one decision, one verdict. One side wins; the other loses. It is always adversarial and you testify on only one side, part of a verbal war of words. Your testimony will be controlled by courtroom procedures, lawyer interventions on both sides, and the circumstances of the case. To further dissipate your testimony, you may be pushed to choose between relative truths. In these ways, the "whole truth" as you know it may not be presented.

LAW AS A WORD WORLD

Most court cases are living examples of the importance of verbal skills—the what, when and how arguments are presented. If the house of law is idea and ideal, words or word usage is the mortar binding the bricks solidly together. Judges and juries decide cases based on what is presented in the context of other similar cases over the years. What is said, when and how presented is of critical importance because they protray and shape what is relevant and irrevelant, true and not true. "There is nothing either good or bad," Shakespeare wrote, "but thinking makes it so" (**Hamlet,** Act II, Scene 2).

As both sides argue and challenge, differences are not so clear between insider trading on Wall Street and everyday business practice, deceptive advertising and a free market, pornography and censorship, resisting arrest and police brutality. In the heat of courtroom conflict, boundaries of what were simple questions before trial become blurred. Was it rape, statutory rape or no crime at all? Medical malpractice or the patient's liability in knowingly assuming risk? What mutual obligations do persons living together assume? The **weight of evidence** is seldom if ever 100 percent but the decision or verdict is a "win" for one side. Plea bargaining is still one verdict, negotiated as it may be.

It is difficult sometimes for judges and juries to determine the criminality or real intent of an act, product safety and the realities of and limitations of quality control, a child's best interests and those of parents. Expert witnesses are interposed between defense and plaintiff, each striving like two wrestlers to gain the advantage, moment by moment as the match continues. This chapter is a compendium of coping and survival tactics to help you "train for the match." Previous chapters described differing perspectives of legal processes from **Alice in Wonderland** idealism and fantasy through "Malice in Wonderland" apprehension and uncertainty about your psychological and emotional survival. This chapter aims at a balance between these two, an enlightened awareness of practical realities but with a firm commitment to speak the truth regardless of its effect and return home after testifying feeling personally satisfied—and professionally proud to contribute to justice, law and truth.

PHYSICAL PREP

Clothing.

Avoid loud clothes and flashy jewelry. Dress tastefully, not flamboyantly. Some experienced expert witnesses recommend you dress like a lawyer. That's generally good advice. Much depends on your occupation and area of expertise. There are distinctive "uniforms" for various occupations. College professors can wear more casual clothing than a bank executive. A highly skilled mechanic can be dressed more informally than a physician, psychiatrist or psychologist. Clothing can add or detract to credibility, strange but true. You should check to see that your jacket is buttoned (shirt and blouse, too, please!), and your shoes clean and polished. A briefcase helps keep your papers together, adds a professional quality to your appearance—and provides a secret place to keep this book for review while waiting to testify.

Posture.

What is your first impression of a person who sits slumped in a chair before you? It is not as favorable as a person who sits erect and so also for you, but do not sit stiffly or on the edge of the chair. That projects the impression you are anxious and tense. A clever opposing lawyer can make that look like apprehension because you're not sure of your facts. Sitting upright suggests you are attentive to what is happening, as you should be. Slouching suggests you're not interested, lazy, indifferent. When you are led by the bailiff to the witness chair, take your seat and take your time arranging needed papers before you. Place both feet flat on the floor. This is called **grounding** or **centering** yourself. You are then "anchored" and "entrenched" physically and this can help you do so psychologically and emotionally.

Your legs should form a 90-degree or right angle. Don't stretch your feet forward! Sometimes your toes will "peep out" from beneath the rail or partition and opposing lawyers can see you nervously moving your feet reacting to their questions. Not as far fetched as it sounds. Give them no free ammunition! If there are arms on the chair, use them. Place your forearms flat on the chair arms, hands should be palms down. This suggests an attentive, receptive, aware attitude and is conducive to it. Getting into a physical **grounded, centered** position has helped many witnesses retain their composure and feelings of stability and security. If the going gets tough as in a searing cross-exaimination, your postural "foundation" will help you be a "fortress" rather than an overrun battle position. It helps you "hold your ground" by having ground to hold on to—the floor and the chair!

Voice.

You should speak in court as you would in any other large public room and in a relaxed tone of voice, at a comfortable rate of speech, and at a volume appropriate to the room size and acoustics. It is helpful to tape-record yourself (audio or video) to help you improve articulation, timing and to eliminate "uhs" and "ahs" and nervous mannerisms such as coughing or clearing your throat. Avoid slang, jargon, excessive use of technical terms, cliches, poor grammer and awkward expressions. Never chew gum or eat candy. Don't drink to "strengthen your nerves" and be aware of the effect of medications you may be taking. Use clear, understandable language in a natural, narrative style. Talk to the judge and jury as equals, colleagues, never condescendingly. It may help you to wet your lips and it's acceptable to ask for a glass of water if you need it. Some women witnesses report they have used this to advantage. Keep gestures to a minimum, preferably not at all.

Prevent Panic and Nervous Mannerisms.

More easily said than done, you say? Again, there are simple physical techniques you can use to prevent your anxiety level from rising to the panic level. First, pay attention to your **breathing rate.** Breathing rate increases in direct proportion to anxiety, so keep your breathing regular. An occasional deep breath helps you to relax, but not frequent deep breaths, because that can lead to hyperventilation, a shortcut to panic. Don't "fiddle" or "play" with anything such as your hair, ring, pin, pencil, paper clip or other objects. Remember Captain Queeg at the **Caine Mutiny Court Martial**? Humphrey Bogart superbly played the captain "cracking up" on the witness stand. He pulled several ball bearings from his pocket and nervously rolled them with his fingers.

If you sit in a swivel chair, don't rock or rotate back and forth Queeg-like. Bogart also looked nervous, avoiding eye contact, looking fearful and anxious. Maintain **optimal eye contact**—neither too much nor too little. Don't glare angrily at the attorney, but don't be a "scared rabbit" either. If it's upsetting for you to look at the opposing attorney or anyone else (it can happen!), look out at the court, in the aisles, at empty seat-backs or the back wall. To the observers, you're still looking **at** and **not away or down.** Remember, you are in court, and while "on the stand" you are very much on "center stage." Your role is that of **an expert**; your appearance and manner and your testimony should fulfill that role.

Arrange notes and papers as soon as you sit down in the witness chair. There is usually a table or desktop, sometimes quite small. Arrange notes and papers for quick access. Don't take too many (shuffling through papers suggests you're not organized, unprofessional). Be prepared for the opposing attorney to ask what you have in front of you and which can be entered into evidence if not previously submitted. If they have not been previously submitted, have enough copies for the inquiring attorney, judge and jury. If challenged, they can be handed out on the spot and the lawyer's "gotcha game" backfires. If you have many papers or articles and books, carry them in a briefcase placed firmly on the floor at your side (right side if right-handed) for easy access when needed. Witnesses with notes and papers before them, ready for testimony and cross-examination suggest an image of a skilled worker with tools of trade at hand, organized, efficient, competent.

Mike Manners.

Most courts today have good acoustics and use microphones and good fidelity speakers. Some witnesses have "mike fright," anxious and fearful when a microphone is placed before them. If your fear is phobic (you have "frozen" speechless in the past) get professional help (relaxation therapy, phobic desensitization, hypnosis). Accept the mike as part of the furniture (it is) and speak in your **normal conversational tone** at at **careful, measured rate of speech** (not too fast, not too slow). Generally, it's better to speak too slowly than too quickly. If you speak rapidly, there is greater chance that listeners cannot "keep up" and understand you. Be aware that as anxiety increases so also does the rate of speech. The opposing attorney may use this to measure how you are reacting to his questioning or claim you're "talking fast to cover up your uncertainty about the facts in this case!" Some people do speak more quickly for this reason. Ralph Waldo Emerson said "when skating over thin ice our safety is in our speed." If there is no microphone, speak up and out and a bit slower than your usual conversational speed. In this way your voice will "fill" the courtroom. With or without a microphone you should listen for your own voice "to come back" or for tiny little silences between voice sounds. Have you ever heard amplified speech spoken so fast that words sound merged together and you couldn't understand what was being said? Use the judge and the two lawyers' rate and volume of speech as a gauge. They've spoken in the same courtroom many times and know the acoustics.

Check yourself out in a mirror for facial expressions and forming words. Try to use your lips a bit more; most people don't. Videotape or audiotape yourself. You won't be thrilled. If you're comfortable with it, rehearse before a friend or a small group of friends. Remind them that "this is serious business." Most friends accept you even when you make little sense and are likely to support you by discounting seriousness or injecting humor. Court **is very serious** and should never be approached lightly. The time for humor and good fellowship is **after the trial—never before.**

MENTAL PREP

Mental preparation for court provides you with the same "anchor to windward" as the physical prepping just described. The **rehearsal** or **practice** aspect is important and should be augmented with mental exercises. In addition to checking yourself out in a mirror and by tape and live practice, go over your testimony aloud while alone and also silently in your mind whenever you have a few minutes. This is especially helpful a week or two before the trial. Some witnesses memorize their initial direct testimony so the wording is exactly what they want to say. It is perfectly ethical to have the attorney requesting your testimony hear this initial statement for any suggestions that will ensure clear, understandable language. Imagine the worst conditions in court and consider how you can best react to them.

Stay Cool.

In addition to the **grounding** and **centering** already described, devise your own "secret weapon" to remain calm and focussed. While it is important to breathe normally, keep feet flat on the floor and arms and hands down and "stable." You can still **release tension** physically by pressing your toes down in your shoes, pressing index fingers to your thumbs or flexing muscles not visible such as in your thighs, calves, buttocks and stomach. Relaxation methods, such as associating an occasional deep breath with a peaceful scene or simply to the idea of relaxation itself, are also not apparent to onlookers. Looking at a nearby object (preferably at or near eye level) can also distract you from obsessive worry, such as the texture, weave, pattern and color of carpeting, the wood grain of a tabletop, the design and color of the microphone before you.

Psych-Check the Courtroom.

As you enter the courtroom, look around, "tuning in" to the size of the room, where judge, jury, lawyers and witness box are located, people seated in the public section and "the media" if present (cameras, reporters with notebooks in hand—usually in the front row). Find comfortable "visual refuges" for your eye if you feel especially tense such as aisles, empty seats, picture, light fixtures, furniture, or interesting, accepting face in the crowd. These visual escape routes should be at or near eye level so that when you look at them it will not appear to be a distant look, daydreaming, preoccupation or boredom but rather similar to good eye contact. An occasional look at the attorney who requested your testimony may evoke an approving nod from him/her and you may arrange for such quick, inconspicuous signals if it will help reassure you and keep you calm. These signals should be done discretely. While it is unlikely the opposing attorney would notice them, since s/he usually faces the court while questioning witnesses; it's possible they could be referred to negatively ("Why are you staring at counsel?" or "Do you need to look to counsel to testify?"). The best strategy is to develop your own internal psychological-emotional techniques to retain your composure and self-confidence.

Be Yourself!

Don't try to role-play some "super expert" fantasy figure or your favorite movie star. Be yourself, and if you can, get a little excited about it! Accept yourself as a human being with the right to live, think and talk about it, and as a citizen with the right to dignity but also, additionally, as an expert with the right to be heard, a professional person. To be only your personal, everyday self may make you more vulnerable under cross-examination if the opposing attorney asks you for a personal opinion. You, of course, should resist answering personal questions not related to your expert testimony. Personal information can be adjudged **hearsay,** inadmissible. Such questions could be a trap to discredit your testimony by drawing you away from your area of expertise.

Still Scared?

Realize, please, that few (if any!) witnesses are as calm in court as when relaxing at home. The same is true for judges and attorneys, even Academy Award actresses and actors. Under some stress, reflexes, reactions and mental processes are quicker, the **fight-or-flight** reaction needed in the Stone Age to survive physical attack and needed as much in the courtroom to survive verbal attack. They can be equally fearful. It's okay to feel apprehensive, anxious, to wonder how you ever got involved, why you ever agreed to testify, to swear solemnly, silently to yourself that you will never **ever,** as long as you live, do it again.

The most experienced expert witness has had those same thoughts and fears before you. As far as we know, no expert witness ever died of fear (or anger) while testifying. You are not alone. Remember, too, that worry is like a rocking chair: it keeps on going but never gets you anywhere! If you owe a bill, worrying about it gives you no discount. If you can't be this philosophical, try examining your feelings of and by themselves, where you feel them (head, stomach, where?) and your earliest memory of such feelings (being punished, horror movie, what?). In this way, you can use your fear to learn more about yourself. Others who have done so have reported that at the next trial they were able to distance themselves more from these annoying feeling. Eventually, they were able to feel them to such a minor degree that they smiled at themselves, at the frightened child they once were many years ago and the now older mature adult who could still feel as a child. It became a warm and postive experience.

PLANNING

Expert witnesses plan for their depositions or court appearances by preparing to provide requested services. For maximum effectiveness, planning should be given the same priority as the actual testimony. Doing so also contributes to greater self-confidence and helps sharpen the focus of expert witness needs and usefulnesss specific to the case. The following are recommended as a checklist to ensure effective planning.

Know What's Needed and Expected.

This stage takes place early, when you are first contacted by the attorney requesting your testimony. At that initial contact you should know precisely what is needed, the type and depth of information and the exact context. If the attorney uses legal terms which are not clear to you, ask for clarification. If you are not familiar with those terms and their applications, research them yourself in a law library (librarians there are very helpful) or other attorneys. You do not gather this information for use in court—the lawyers do that—but so that you will better understand your function as an expert witness.

Study Your Work, Report or Statement, and Notes.

In this area, you alone are the expert. The lawyers can't really help except to ask or suggest what is relevant to the case. Be able to clearly and simply rephrase this material. A major complaint about experts is the use of specialized vocabulary, jargon or gibberish. A clever opposing attorney can use excessive use of technical terms against you. You **are** an authority and should look and sound like one, but not at the price of losing credibility because no one understands you.

Focus on Main Points.

Keep in mind "the bottom line" which is the "heart" of your testimony, the major points which in your judgment best answer the questions raised or address informational needs. If it will help, try preparing a clearly typed, one-page, one-side summary sheet of these main points, and remember to have copies for the judge, clerk and lawyers if asked what that is before you.

Consult with counsel, the lawyer requesting your testimony, as to how you fit into the case, some idea of her/his major points. If you do not, in the heat of cross-examination you could be moved off on tangents not relevant to your testimony but which support defendant or plaintiff sides of the case. Plan your testimony like a military campaign: far easier to plan in advance. Some lawyers provide time for consultation before trial and even help experts with a "mock cross-examination." Be prepared, though, for an opposing lawyer's questioning as to the nature and extent of your meetings with "your" attorney or the charge that your testimony is "rehearsed and coached by counsel and therefore biased."

PERFORMANCE TIPS

1. Be Comfortable Saying, "I don't know."

No one can know everything. If you attempt answers to any and all questions, the opposing attorney can use this against you by leading you off on a tangent, then exposing inconsistencies. You are then out on a limb with an eager lawyer, saw in hand! If you're not certain, it's okay to say so and you should say so. An expert does not have to know **everything**.

2. Avoid Using the Lawyer's Same Words.

This could be a trick, a tactic of reframing what you say in the opposing lawyer's words used throughout the trial to support defendant or plaintiff claims. Instead, rephrase, reflect, reframe **in your words,** or with the words of your profession or occupation, to preserve the integrity of your testimony (and your own personal integrity).

3. Confronted With "Iffy" Question, Ask For More Information.

If your opinion is asked, it should be based on a clear understanding of the question—and what may be implied in it. Generally, the question gets simpler as you ask for more details, and the questioner sees that you're thinking through your answers and may back off and try another tactic.

4. Never Accept Unfamiliar Data.

This, too, can be a trap to distort or discredit your testimony. If asked: "Are you familiar with the 1987 study of Schnodgrass and Bunion at Harvard?" and are not familiar with it, say so. Be prepared for: "Many consider this to be a major contribution. Isn't it strange you don't know about it?" If it **is** so major, you should know about it. If it isn't, make that point. You could offer to read it and render an opinion—but not on the stand with only a few minutes to do so. If it's that important, you're justified in asking for more time to review it.

5. Pause Before Answering Questions.

This gives "your" attorney time to object if doing so is warranted. In this way poorly worded leading or hypothetical questions can be rephrased. If an opposing lawyer tries to shorten your reaction time ("You seem to pause and hestitate—does this mean you're uncertain of your opinion?") you could reply: "These are important questions and I want to answer them carefully" or words to that effect.

6. Don't Be Evasive.

If you're not certain, say so directly. To hedge or evade suggests you are uncertain—or, worse still for an expert witness, devious. If you can't be specific, explain why.

7. Take Your Time.

Answer slowly, carefully, to set an easier pace for yourself and (really) to give yourself more reaction and thinking time if you need it. If the opposing lawyer "pushes" too much, the friendly attorney should object: "Objection! Counsel is badgering the witness" or similar intent. If you are being "skewered" without objection and it's **really bad,** you can turn to the judge and ask for more time to respond. Most lawyers do not like witnesses involving the judge (they fear the judge as witnesses fear lawyers). But avoid this radical action; use it only if you really feel you must. You might want to discuss this with counsel before trial. If you do use it, don't overdo it and look like "a shrinking violet" or one overly sensitive because you aren't sure of your opinion.

8. Don't Overanswer.

Provide just enough information. Don't overkill. If you need to explain more than you have and really feel it is a key point, "your" lawyer can continue your testimony later. Hopefully, the lawyer requesting your testimony and you have gone over your testimony to the extent that s/he will know what is and is not important. It really depends on the lawyer's judgment and priorities, not yours. What may be important to you can be less important and not at all critical to the attorney. Worse still, the more you say the more opposing attorneys have at their disposal to use against you: "All human beings, including experts, are also liable to use inartful phrases or words upon occasion. Infelicitous phrases in an expert's written report are unnecessary holes below his waterline" (Chu, 1982, page 64).

SURVIVAL TACTICS

Hypothetical Questions/Situations.

There are few trials without the use of hypothetical cases or questions posed by attorneys on both sides. "What if" they ask, waiting for the "then" conclusion, for which they may have other questions leading to discrediting some or all of what you have said. Be very careful what you concede and be aware of word usage and the hypothetical facts. You don't have to play the game: "That's a hypothetical situation and I prefer not to speculate on it. I would need much more information than you have given and more time to consider it in the context of my area of expertise, as I have done in this case." Or "such a situation is complex and there are many variables to be considered, each with a definite effect or influence on conclusions to be made." Or "if you're referring to this case,

I am willing to reconsider my opinion if you have new information." Be respectful not sarcastic or condescending.

Leading Questions.

Sharpen your awareness of assumptions, generalizations, and oversimplifications. Do this in your everyday life by listening to conversations, TV news summaries, and newspaper editorials. In court, answer general questions generally—and say so ("Generally . . .). As the questions become more specific, so too should your answers. Spot and "call" a generalization as it arises ("That's a generalization and there are exceptions . . . " or similar). If you agree with one generalization it can lead to another, escalate, and you find yourself out on that limb again.

Layer Cake.

This lawyer's tactic is to ask you several questions at one time, like a layer cake: "Well, if A is B and H were F, would X be Z? It's (deliberately) confusing, a veritable verbal minefield. If it's a dazzling array and you feel uncertain, unable to put all the questions into enough perspective to answer, it's perfectly acceptable to say so. If you do understand all the "layers," answer one at a time and take your time doing so. Take notes as the question is asked if it will help (can't hurt). As questions become more complex, answers should reflect the complexity (more difficult to answer a simple yes or no). Many experts have found it useful to ask the lawyer to restate "layer cake" questions. In most cases, the question becomes simpler. If you ask details or for a second repeat, it is likely the question will become more manageable!

Avoid "Yes" or "No" Tracking.

An opposing attorney may try to "track" you with yes-or-no answers, their last questions being "the stinger" which changes your testimony or favors their side. Questions may lead from fact to theory, moving you to "thin ice" areas, the final "yes" or "no" sawing off that damned limb again! If questions can't be answered precisely with yes or no, use other words: "In most cases . . . sometimes . . . that depends . . . that's generally true." Beware of exceptions. Lawyers will use them to discredit what is generally true. If there is one exception, they are likely to use it to challenge your opinion. Here presence of mind is needed, based on your planning and physical and mental preparation.

"Would It" or "Could It" Questions.

These are variations of the yes-no tracking described above and somewhat similar to the hypothetical "What if . . . then . . . . " These questions usually start with: "Would it change your opinion if . . . " or "What would it take to change your opinion?" This question can precede a "bombshell" surprise such as "Would it change your opinion about this product's safety to know it is illegal to sell it in 23 states and has been the subject of many damage suits?" You should, of course, know about such things before the trial, from the attorney requesting your testimony. If the question involves hypothetical and not factual circumstances, prepare for it as described in the preceding paragraph.

Doom's Day!

Imagine the worst turn of events and prepare for it. This will become your "emergency snakebite kit" or "worst case scenario" survival plan. It doesn't matter what is the cause. Your rehearsed, memorized automatic response for any situation should be the same. It will give you time to form a reasoned response to the specific attack fully reflecting your expertise, not just a personal, emotional defensive reaction. Well in advance of every trial you should carefully choose the wording, tone of voice, and speed of delivery which is natural for you. It is **imperative** that you do this before the trial, because if you're "ambushed" in court you will be suddenly plunged into a severe stress situation. Discuss the possibility of such a situation with the lawyer requesting your testimony and get some advice as to the preferred way you should cope with it. Use your own wording, something like: "No, I was not aware of that. If it is true and as you have stated it I would want to review my opinion, my written report and previous testimony" or if this is yielding too much, "I feel I need more time to consider this important information. I don't feel prepared at this moment to render an opinion on it."

Direct Attack.

This is a histrionic outburst by opposing counsel who yells, screams and harangues you. Usually, the attorney is fully aware of his/her behavior and it's a tactic to move you from an opinion or your wording in giving an opinion. It's a search for a "chink in your armor." The same question can be reworded: "And you are saying to this court that . . . " or "and you insist that in your opinion . . . . " It is very important that you retain your composure. If you get apologetic or rattled, it can be used against you: "I note a change in your voice now (or your demeanor). Does this mean you realize you may have been mistaken?" If you have planned and prepared yourself, with the summary sheet before you, you should in a calm voice respond. Some suggested wording: "Perhaps I was not clear in giving my opinion that . . . " or "I can only repeat to you my opinion that . . . . " Be careful not to sound sarcastic. "I've already testified on that point" can be a calm, reasoned response or defensive and antagonistic.

You should develop a psychological and emotional defense to protect you against hurt feelings. When someone yells at you, even if they are 100 percent wrong and you know it's a legal maneuver, feelings can be hurt. Reflect on this in advance, rationalizing it for what it is, that it is not personal. It might help to think of how much like a matador you must be, to sidestep the charging bull, or how such behavior "hooks into" childhood memories of being reprimanded by a parent or teacher. Develop these defenses in advance so you will be "inoculated" beforehand and far less subject to the panic reaction of sudden attack.

Sarcasm (from the opposing attorney)

Some lawyers may use sarcasm or ridicule to the same end as the direct attack just described. When subjected to this humiliating put-down, it is important that you do not answer in a similar fashion. That means two "beasts from the dark lagoon" loose in the courtroom. If you can't beat 'em, don't join 'em. You are an expert and that means you are there to provide a public service, more as a friend of the court than an adversary. If treated like an adversary, you can and should respond with dignity and integrity. I have always had a secret saying whenever an attorney uses direct attack or sarcasm: "Be kind to dumb animals." Anyone behaving in such an unkind manner is much like a "dumb animal." So give the animals a break, ignore the tone and words, and respond as if there was no attack. Be gracious. Let your behavior contrast the "beast's." In this way the sarcasm can backfire and kill the monster!

Belittling; Needling.

This occurs when the questions have a built-in insult to you: "I respect your opinion but want to point out that Doctor Satchelbottom has a lot more education, training and experience than you." The reference can be to an expert from another field, such as a design engineer against an appliance repairman in a product liability case, a psychiatrist against a social worker or pastoral counselor, a retired FBI agent against a county deputy sheriff. Be yourself and reflect your own expertise—that's why you're there. "In my experience . . . " and restate your opinion. Never attack or belittle the other experts. That only discredits **all experts** and that includes you.

Rapid-Fire Questions.

This is the "machine gun" delivery of questions, one after another, with little or no time between them. When used it is an intentional tactic to push you into admitting what is not or is only partially true. You should never answer with the same speed (which will increase). Instead, slow down your responses and use "braking" words such as: "Well, in my opinion . . . in such a case . . . in that context . . . stated that way." Don't be evasive. Answer the questions, to the best of your knowledge and ability (as always!) but in a measured, comfortable rate of speed. You can build in "stops" or pauses with: "I would need more informaiton to answer that" or "Do you mean . . . " or "What exactly do you mean by . . . . " If the lawyer comments on your slowing down as a possible sign of uncertainty, response as noted earlier: "These are important questions and I want to carefully consider my answers to them."

Whatcha Got There?

This can be a genuine effort by an opposing lawyer to ensure that all evidence is before the court or another tactic to raise your anxiety level and increase stress and pressure to make you more pliable. The lawyer can walk up close to you in the witness chair, bend over and dramatically point with finger to your notes: "What's this? Have these papers been admitted into evidence? Does the court have them?" If you're not prepared for such a question, the effect can be unsettling to you. It has nothing to do with your testimony, doesn't change it at all, but is just another technique used to exert pressure on you. As has been pointed out earlier in this chapter, it is helpful to have a summary sheet of the major points of your testimony there before you, with copies if challenged. You should respond with your own words but something like: "This is a brief summary of the major points of my testimony." Be prepared for further questions such as "Who wrote them for you?" or "Did you write that after discussing the case with counsel?" This is an attempt to show you were biased by your discussions with the attorney requesting your testimony or that s/he coached you as to what to say.

So What Do You Think?

This is rarely used but is a question to you about the totality of the case: "So what do you think the judge (or jury) should decide in this case?" It's a legal question, one for the trier of fact, the judge or jury, not for any witness, expert or other. Your duty and obligation is to provide information not otherwise available and any opinion based on the information which is relevant to the case. You should not have an opinion as to outcome except as may develop indirectly throughout the trial. Your answer, then, should be something like: "I have no opinion on that . . . " or "That's for this court to decide . . . . "

The Pacer.

This is an attorney who walks back and forth across the courtroom as s/he asks you questions. If it's a jury trial, this may be a tactic to divert your eye contact from the jury. It may be simply a further effort to keep you **moving,** to distract you, together with other unsettling tactics such as sarcasm or histrionic behaviors (gesturing, yelling, intentional pauses, looks or disdain). I have always found such behaviors ludicrous and humorous, but one must be careful never to smile or laugh. On one occasion, the attorney got even more upset and yelled louder, claiming I had no respect for the court or legal process. He was only partially correct! You've got to tolerate these behaviors. As has been said here, never try to "one up" them at the same game. Lawyers have a lot more freedom in court than a witness. It's their world and you are as in "Star Trek" "just visiting this planet."

Learned Treatise.

This is to be presented in court with what seems to be an authoritative reference. It can be a book or journal article or someone else's report from another case, a speech or newsletter or magazine. You can usually "see it coming" on the lawyer's desk or in hand when questions are asked. Regardless of that source, there are key factors that influence its significance, importance, even its validity: and there are date or recency, authorship, scope and context (same kind of information, same people, use) and how much is being quoted. In most cases only a sentence or paragraph are quoted—clearly out of context. Any "learned treatises" should be put into perspective, especially if there are more recent references even more relevant to the case.

Dirty Tricks.

There are many subtle and not so subtle "put-downs" used to discredit your opinion:

Sexism. Male voices are deeper than females, and males also have larger lungs. Male lawyers can speak loudly, reverberating through the courtroom, and the female witness responds with a softer voice which by contrast sounds "less strong" suggesting less credibility. Some male lawyers will avoid titles ("Doctor") and use "Miss" or "Ms" even though a male exert is called "Doctor." A woman who insists on her rightful title can sound (too) assertive and this may adversely affect credibility. Women should make known to the attorney requesting their testimony how they want to be identified. In this way one lawyer can correct the other without adverse effect on the witness's testimony.

"Are You Published in This Field?" is a favorite question when you are not published and an expert on the other side is. It adds to your credibility to have publications. Actually, it does nothing for the **admissibility** of your testimony, but it does definitely add to the **weight** of your testimony. If you aren't published, simply answer "no" and let it go at that. Some experts have responded: "No, but I have taught (or represented at some professional conference) . . . . "

"How Many Cases Like This Have You Seen?" or "How Many Times Have You Testified in Court in Similar Cases?" You can only answer this factually. Technically, no two cases are identical. They can be similar, but it is very rare that they would be identical. But this is a matter to be clarified between the lawyers and decided by judge or jury.

"Isn't What You Do More Art Than Science?" or **"You're Just a Skilled Workman, a Technician."** Here again, all you can do is refer to your education, knowledge, training, skills and experience. Mental health professionals are often asked about **art** and **science** and the desired answer is **art** so their testimony can be discounted as unscientific. Many experts yield and concede that what they do is more art than science. Skilled workers and technicians can provide more information relevant to product liability than the professionals who designed the product and those who manufactured it. There can be defects unforseen in design or manufacture. That's why we have test pilots and testing grounds for automobiles.

Theoretical Bias. This is an attempt to show that what you do or what you have been doing has in some way influenced your opinion. Your response should point out the truth of your background and any effect which **could have** resulted from it to alter your opinions. If it has not, you should say so but not in any defensive way to suggest that you **really are** biased and are reacting to discovery of that fact. "You've been working for Factory X for 20 years. Do you think you can be objective in an opinion about their products?" Or: "You are a graduate of Y School, famous for their support of Theory A. Can you be objective in your opinion about Theory A or the widgets made from applying that theory?" This is a clever attempt to discredit what you say even before you say it!

"Your Examination/Interview/Inspection/Report was Brief and Superficial." This attempts to discredit your opinion as based on insufficient data, limited by time and therefore depth. Describe the nature of your observations, the basis of your findings.

"You Got Paid for Your Opinion, Didn't You?" The factual answer is "yes," in that you were paid for the work you did in the case, but a "yes" implies "you were bought." The best way to respond is something like: "I was paid for my services, not for my opinion." Your findings would be the same regardless of who paid for them, correct? Of course, otherwise you are not an expert witness but an advocate for one of the two sides.

"Did You Read Other Experts' Reports?" or **"Did You Read Anything About This Case From Any Source?"** Certainly all sources of data are helpful—but lawyers who use this ploy attempt to discredit your opinion because it **could have** been based on or influenced by what you read in other sources. This is the same kind of "attack" used to disqualify jurors who may have read descriptions of the case in the newspapers or learned details on radio or TV. You should respond in your own words, but here is a suggestion: "I find information helpful regardless of source or opinion. My opinion was based on my own examination/inspection/observation after reviewing all available material, mine and others."

Do You Ever Make Mistakes?
Could You Be Making a Mistake Now?

The only reasonable, logical reply to the first question is "yes." But that is used as a wedge, a "foot in the door," for the second question. The opposing attorney, having established that you can and do make mistakes and admit it, attempts to generalize this, magnify and exaggerate it to cast doubt on your entire testimony. Note that the questions have nothing to do with the content of your testimony. They're "off the wall," really an **ad hominem** attack to discredit all you say because in some certain limited situations you can and do make mistakes. The answer to the second question should be "no." Be prepared for these questions and be able to differentiate between "making mistakes" as a general proposition to specific mistakes in your testimony.

Use your own language, but your response should point out that mistakes are not likely in situations which are important (such as court) and that you proceeded with more than average care. If the attorney persists, such as: "But you admit that you make mistakes and if you do it is possible that you have made mistakes in your evaluation, report or in your testimony, isn't that reasonable?" You must then decide whether to meet this argument head-on. I do: "No, I don't agree. Because of the importance I place on testifying in court, it is to me reasonable that I made no mistakes." Other experts have replied: "I'm willing to further examine and review anything I've said or written point by point if you feel there are mistakes there."

"Maybe He/She/It Behaved That Way Just For You." Whatever you did as an expert witness to study a person, product or situation should have included other sources of information and not simply your own. "I would concede the possibility that someone can be influenced by what is read or said to him/her, but in this case: I used a variety of sources and reviewed data of others as well as my own to form an opinion."

What's Your Horsepower? This is not a question you'll be asked in these words, of course, but there are many little "needles" that can be figuratively stuck into you to diminish the weight of your testimony, such as the following:

- Lack of license or certificate;
- Years of experience (while it's unacceptable to ask your age, questions about experience can suggest that you're "young and inexperienced");
- Years of education. An M.D. is, at this writing, "heavier" than a Ph.D.; a Ph.D. in the "chess game" of witness credibility "takes" a master's or bachelor's degree.
- Comparative occupations. A CPA is more credible than an accountant; FBI or state police officers more than city or county officers; professors more than teachers; legislators more than individual citizens.
- Publications, professional memberships, awards and honors, appointive and elective officers in a profession or occupation, are all plus factors, especially if testifying against an expert without them.

CONCLUSION

This chapter may be upsetting to you. You may feel it is an overreaction by an aging expert from too many years of courtroom combat, that lawyers "don't do things like that." Not all of them do but **most will** if your testimony is important enough to one side and therefore dangerous and threatening to the other. As testimony increases in importance so also does the likelihood of "catching hell" in court.

Ostroff (1982) urged his fellow lawyers to "depose the opposing experts" and advised them how to "read every publication by them . . . point out any inconsistencies . . . prior depositions and trial testimony . . . transcripts of his grades . . . evaluations of him from professors and peers." Ostroff concedes experts "almost always know more about his field than will trial counsel" and so "collateral or **ad hominem** attacks may be the only available avenue of cross-examination." He concludes that "if there is a blot somewhere on the expert's record, you need to know it to protect or attack the witness" (p. 9).

But Ostroff also offers expert witnesses some practical, positive advice: "Experts should exude competence and credibility . . . telegraphed by their clothing and appearance, careful preparation and rehearsal" and who "speaks without condescension, arrogance or pomposity . . . admits when he is uncertain, acknowledges he has erred in the past and doubtless will in the future and concedes indisputable facts even when they are adverse . . . cannot be goaded into taking positions he has not considered carefully before assuming the witness stand" (p. 9).

It is hoped this chapter will provide you with a "stress inoculation" that by being forewarned you are forearmed and better equipped to withstand whatever will come in the "wrestling match" of the trial process. Despite the negatives, even if your "worst case scenario" becomes an **underestimate,** the ideals described in Chapter 2 remain. They will be there as a candle in the night in your darkest hour in court. You may want to read that chapter again or skim through it, especially if you're feeling a bit cynical right now. Your duty as an expert witness remains to inform the court despite the obstacles portrayed here. I have never been subjected to all or many of the tactics described in this chapter in one trial. They are more likely to occur from time to time with random incidence.

Testifying as an expert witness can (and will be) satisfying or it can (and will occasionally be) unsettling or frightening, pleasant or unpleasant or a bittersweet blend (like life!). Ralph Waldo Emerson could have just as well described the "life and times of a courtroom witness" when he wrote: "Every sweet has its sour; every evil its good" (**Compensation,** in **Essays, First Series**). If you prepare for all the sweets and all the sours, there is no doubt you will be strong enough to survive any courtroom combat situation.

MY FINAL SUMMATION

The best expert witnesses are stout-hearted, thick-skinned and quick-witted. In the Stone Age they would be among the survivors. Today, they believe in law as idea and ideal. That is as evolutionary and ideal as it is revolutionary. They believe that they can make a difference by testifying and providing information needed by the triers of fact to more clearly see the truth. To me, being an expert witness is a civic duty every bit as much as jury duty. It is also an ethical obligation, whatever one's career or profession. It is not unlike law as a sacred trust and noble calling. May it be so for you. I leave you with three special blessings, messages I wish I had when I began my expert witness services in the early 1970s. I offer them to help reassure you, to bolster your self-confidence:

1. As you prepare yourself, as you prepare your materials, prepare, too, to be the best expert witness you can by doing the best you can. As our good friend Ralph Waldo Emerson said, "Make the most of yourself—that's all there is of you!" And heed the **rule** of John Wesley (1703-1791):

   Do all the good you can,
   By all the means you can,
   In all the ways you can,
   In all the places you can,
   At all the times you can,
   To all the people you can,
   As long as ever you can.

2. As you look back on what you've done, these words of an old Alaskan sourdough may be helpful:

   I ain't what I wanna be.
   I ain't what I'm gonna be.
   But I sure as hell
   Ain't what I used to be!

3. Though we've never met face to face, you and I, we have shared this book together. It's my hope that you feel better prepared, more relaxed with the legal process, than if you hadn't read it. Farewell, friend and colleague, go with this my final blessing to you:

May your time in court be brief
And the lawyers kind;
May you return home unscathed,
Feel satisifed, glad you served,
Your duty done and done well.
May you sleep well that night,
And all the nights to come.
May your life and your spirit
Continue all the better for it!

Good luck!

REFERENCES

MacHovec, F. J. (1984). *Courtroom survival.* Danville, VA: Author.

GLOSSARY

Abandon; abandonment: intent to or the external act of deserting; forsaking or relinquishing a right or interest or failing to fulfil a contract with no intention of resuming right or interest; used in malpractice and negligence cases; when it is charged a person needing care or services is denied them; also used in cases of child custody, divorce, water or mineral rights, property and contracts, copyright, trademarks, inventions and patents.

Abet (Fr., **abeter,** to bait or excite animals): Aiding, inciting or encouraging someone to commit crime; includes "guilty knowledge" or awareness of wrongful pupose of the perpetrator of a crime.

Abjure (L., **Abjurare,** to swear): To renounce a right or privilege under oath such as renouncing one's citizenship.

Abrogate (L., **Abrogatus,** to ask or propose): to repeal, annul, such as a law by legislative action or a lower court's order by a higher court; **implied abrogation** occurs when laws newly enacted contradict (**abrogate**) older laws, rendering the older laws unnecessary.

Abscond (L., **abscondere,** to hide): A conscious, deliberate attempt to evade or avoid legal process, law or a court's jurisdiction usually by absenting one's self (hiding or running away).

Absente; in absentia (L., absent): not there; **absente reo** is when the defendant is absent.

Abuse (L., **abusus,** to consume): That which is contrary to and departs from good faith, reasonable care or usage, is excessive or improper or physically or mentally harmful such as **alcohol, drug, child, spouse,** or **sexual abuse**; to malign, disparage or revile another (**verbal abuse**); legal or judicial errors (**abuse of discretion; abuse of process**).

NOTE: This glossary is intended for prospective witnesses or expert witnesses so that they can better understand and more effectively participate in the trial process. Definitions and applications of law vary state to state, state to federal and with the type of court, and a local attorney should be consulted for more definitive explanation and practical applications of the terms and concepts which are included in this glossary.

Accessory (L., **accessus,** to approach): A person who directly or indirectly assists in committing a crime; to assist a felon escape arrest (**accessory after the fact**); to instigate and encourage someone to commit a crime (**accessory before the fact**).

Accomplice (L., **complicare,** to associate with): One who knowingly and willingly joins with or assists, aids or abets another to commit a crime.

Accrue (L., **ad creso,** to increase): To increase or vest as in profit and interest; to come into existence as when the cause of legal action **accrues** on the date of injury or damage, not when causative factors began.

Accumulative sentence; consecutive sentence: Prison sentences for more than one crime to be served in sequence, thus accumulating.

Acknowledge: To admit, concede, avow, confess one's acts; to do so establishes legal responsibility.

Acquit; acquittal (L., **aquiter,** free of): To absolve, release or free from liability, guilt or legal responsibility.

Act (L., **actus,** a doing, an act): The external manifestation of intent, will or purpose, by commission or omission, in public or in private; implies the act was voluntary, required proof in criminal law.

Actio (L., action): Legal action or right, **actio civilo** if civil, **actio criminalis** if criminal, **actio in personem** personal liability, **actio ex deicto** or **actio ex maleficio** for torts or personal injury, **actio in rem** to recover a right or property, or **actio ex contractu** for contractual claims.

Action (L., **actio,** action): What is done or acte dout; formal complaint; counterclaim or lawsuit; behavior or conduct.

Actionable: When grounds for legal proceedings are satisfied.

Act of God; Act of Providence: The effect or result solely of natural, physical causes independent and exclusive of human involvement and which neither foresight nor reasonable care or skill could prevent.

Actuarial table: A statistical data-base listing life expectancies, admissible as evidence and usually presented by an expert witness such as an insurance company **actuary.**

Actus reus (L., guilty deed): Wrongful act or guilty deed; with **ments rea** (guilty mind) criminal liability is established.

Ad damnum (L., for damage): Plaintiff's claim for monetary damage.

Adequate care: Care which **a reasonable person** would expect in similar circumstances and proportionate to the risk involved.

Adequate notice: Reasonable and sufficient scheduling to allow for filing papers, discovery, arranging for witnesses, research and preparing arguments.

Ad hoc (L., for this): For a special purpose, in a specified situation.

Ad hominem (L., against the person): An attack on personal characteristics, subjective factors, rather than on what is said on its own merits, such as appearance, attitude, mannerisms, occupation, marital status, political affiliation, even age, sex, race, religion, social class or national origin.

Ad infinitum (L., to infinity): Limitless, infinite, ongoing indefinitely, without stated or implied end.

Adjudicate; adjudication (L., **adjudicare,** to judge): To complete formal legal proceedings and deliberation by pronouncing judgment or issuing an order or decree.

Ad litem, guardian (L., for the suit): Legally authorized representative or guardian of an incapacitated or an incompetent person unable to testify on his or her own behalf.

Administrative Law Judge: A judge presiding at an administrative hearing who is authorized to give oaths, take testimony, weigh evidence and determine fact, such as Social Security disability appeals hearings.

Admissible evidence: Evidence which satisfies applicable rules and laws.

Admonition (L., **admonitio,** friendly warning): In court, when the judge advises, instructs or cautions the jury as to what is and is not admissible or about their duties, conduct or alternatives of verdict; also when a judge warns a defendant or convicted felon of the consequences for future misconduct or when a judge cautions or reprimands an attorney.

Adversary; adverse party (L., **adversus,** against): Person(s) who comprise the opposing side in a case; opponent(s).

Adversary system: Trial process from ancient to present time requiring defense and plaintiff to argue their case monitored by an impartial judge or jury (**trier of fact**) who decides which side proves their claim.

Adverse witness: Witness on the side opposing the lawyer questioning that witness; used also to refer to a **hostile witness,** one whose testimony is not favorable to the side which requested that witness.

Advice of counsel: A lawyer's advice to a client; a defendant's claim s/he followed counsel's advice in good faith; used sometimes to justify declining to testify on grounds to do so may tend to incriminate ("pleading the Fifth Amendment").

Advocate (L., **advocatus,** to summon): A lawyer who advises, defends, files claims and pleads cases thus **advocating** for clients.

Affidavit (L., **affidare,** to swear to): Documented, sworn, voluntary declaration or statement of fact.

Affirmation (L., **affirmare,** to make firm): When a person declines to swear an oath (usually because of religious conviction) and a formal, solemn **affirmation** is substituted. The person usually says " I affirm" instead of "I swear" with or without "so help me God" or placing a hand on the Bible.

Affirmative defense: A defense strategy of stating a reason, explanation or justification to satisfy claims or neutralize charges, such as **contributory negligence** or **assumption of risk** by plaintiff, **irresistible impulse** or **insanity** for defendant in criminal cases (**NGI**).

Age: There are by law **ages of entitlement** or **ages of responsibility** for rights and liability such as marrying without parental permission (**age of consent**), child not competent to testify in court nor liable for a crime (**age of reason**), to vote, drink, adopt children, sole self support, hold office or title to property (**age of majority**).

Agent (L., **agere,** to lead, act or do): A person who is authorized by another to act for and represent her or him.

Aggravated assault: Attempted or completed bodily injury purposely inflicted, with or without use of **a deadly weapon** or **intent to kill,** or injury caused by recklessness or indifference.

Aggravated battery: The use of excessive force to physically attack someone.

Aggravation (L., **aggravatus,** to make heavier): The relative force or violence and its potential for serious injury or death, a factor which adds to the seriousness of the crime.

Agreement (L., **gratus,** pleasing): Mutual understanding and shared intentions toward a common goal usually by written contract, involving rights, property, duties, performance, obligations and benefits. They are **conditional** if based on conditions or contingencies, **executed** if based on past performance, **executory** if on future performance, **express** if terms are specified at the time of contract, or **implied** or **quasi** if unstated or unwritten, based on the prior record and character of the contracting parties.

Aid (L., **adjutare,** to help): To assist, support, cooperate with another in the commission of a crime, usually by material means, as distinguished from **abet** which is nonmaterial, to counsel, encourage or incite in the commission of a crime. **To aid and abet** combines these two factors.

Aid and comfort: Relates to the crime of **treason** when a person knowingly and willingly supports and strengthens enemies of the state (government) or increases the likelihood of hostile acts by enemies.

Alias; a.k.a. (L., **alias dictus,** otherwise named or known): To be known by another name, a fictitious name.

Alibi (L., **alius,** elsewhere): A defense proving the defendant was not present at the scene and time of the crime thus invalidating criminal charges.

Alienation of affection: A **tort action** (civil case) charging unjustified, malicious interference in a marriage by a third person resulting in diminishing or loss of affection of the spouse.

Allegation (L., **allegare,** to cite): A charge, claim or assertion which forms the basis for litigation; declaration or statement of grounds for action and legal proofs to be demonstrated in court.

Amicus curiae (L., friend of the court): A third party requested by defense or plaintiff to provide information relevant to the case.

Analogy (L., **analogus,** ratio, reason): A similar (**analogous**) event, situation or relationship to that which is being litigated; reasoning by analogy.

Answer (Old English, **andswaru,** to reply): Written response from defense to the plaintiff's complaint admitting or denying allegations and stating counterarguments.

A posteriori (L., from effect to cause): An inductive argument using recent knowledge, experience or observations as effect and the result of a preceding cause.

Appeal (Middle English, **appelen,** to move or drive toward): Review by a higher court requested by the defense in the hope of reversing the lower court decision.

Appear (Middle English, **apperen,** to show one's self): To be physically present and thus legally accounted for.

Appelant (L., **appelatus,** who asks for): One who **appeals,** who requests higher court review of a case.

Appelant court: State or federal courts that receive, review then confirm or reverse lower court decisions.

Appelate court: State or federal courts that receive, review then confirm or reverse lower court decisions.

Appelee (or **respondent**): Party opposing an appeal; the adversary in an appeal.

Approbation (L., **approbatus,** approve): Approval, commendation.

A priori (L., cause to effect): Deductive argument, from cause, an accepted truth or established principle, to effect the consequent result; an argument based on tradition and precedent.

Arbitrary; arbitrary and capricious: Unreasonable, unprincipled, unfair, not done in good faith, based on will and impulse.

Arbitration (L., **arbiter,** to render judgment): Settling differences by submitting to a hearing by a court-appointed impartial **arbiter** or **arbitrator,** having agreed to accept her/his conclusions; **divorce mediation** is a form of agreed arbitration using a therapist which avoids the cost and potentially bitter courtroom confrontation.

Argument (L., **argumentum,** argument): Presentation by a lawyer to persuade judge or jury by facts and inferences, grounds or defense, of the merits of a case.

Arraignment (Old English, **arreinen,** to speak up): In criminal law, the pretrial process of reading charges or an indictment to the defendant in open court to which s/he **pleads guilty** or **not guilty** or, if permissible, **nolo contendere.**

Art, words of: Descriptive, specialized scientific or technical vocabulary; the verbal "best fit" to describe something. Much expert witness testimony contains **words of art.**

Assault (L., **assaltus,** to attack): With or without physical contact or touch, a willful attempt or threat to injure by pointing, using or threatening to use a weapon (**assault with a deadly weapon**) or if sufficient to cause death but the victim survived (**assault with intent to cause manslaughter**) or with **malice aforethought** and intent to kill (**assault with intent to commit murder**) or **assault with intent to commit rape** when there is evidence to substantiate the charge. **Battery** always requires physical contact, from unlawful touching to forceful striking. (See also **Aggravated assault; Aggravated battery.**)

Assent (L., **assentare,** to sense or feel): To approve, confirm, agree to, comply with.

Assigns; assignees (L., **assignare,** to mark or sign): Person(s) to whom property can be transferred (**assigned**).

Assumption of risk: Legal doctrine that a plaintiff cannot recover damages for injury when risk was known, understood and accepted beforehand.

At issue: When defense and plaintiff reach the point of irreconcilable difference and when the basis of the litigation is evident.

Attachment: Seizing or taking custody of a person or property by court order, summons or writ to satisfy a claim or judgment.

Attest (L., **attestare,** to witness): To affirm or state unequivocally that something is true; one who signs to identify and validate a document is **an attesting witness.**

Attorney (L., **ad torner,** one who turns): Legal representative authorized to act on behalf of another, for a specific purpose or lawful act (**attorney of fact**), by written authorization (**power of attorney; letter of attorney**) or who receives, prepares, responds to and formally files legal papers pleads cases and is named in the court transcript (**attorney of record**).

Attorney's lien (L., **ligamen,** to bind): An attorney's written claim of the right to be paid for legal services rendered.

Attractive nuisance: Legal doctrine that where there is a potentially dangerous situation that may attract children **of tender years,** there is a duty to take precautions which **a reasonably prudent person** would take to prevent injury.

Authentication (L., **authenticua,** masterful): Steps taken to validate evidence, to certify it as **admissible,** that it is what it is claimed to be and proven to the satisfaction of the court; statute books, notarized documents and certified copies are admitted without proof (**self-authenticated**) but other evidence is of lesser authenticity and subject to question, objection or further verification.

Authoritative (L., **auctoritas,** decision power or opinion): The validity of a source of information such as a (text)book or article or other **standard reference**. To accept a source as **authoritative** is to accept it in its entirety and without exception.

Aver (L., **ad verus,** very true): To formally assert, affirm, declare.

Average man/person test: When a prospective juror claims to be free to bias but is actually so involved with the case that **the average person** in the same situation would likely be biased and unaware of it, the juror can be **disqualified** despite her/his contention.

Avow (L., **advocare,** to firmly declare): To declare, justify, acknowledge.

Award (Middle English, **awarden,** to decide): To **pass sentence** or make judgment, to grant, assign, adjudge, confer.

Bad character: Of such negative or evil character as to lessen credibility.

Bad debt: Uncollectible, unpaid bill or fee.

Bad faith (L., **mala fides**): Intent to mislead, deceive or defraud; knowingly and willingly neglecting or refusing to fulfill a duty or responsibility; **bad faith** is beyond **negligence** because of conscious evil intent.

Badges of fraud: Deliberate evasion, false statements, unusual or suspicious circumstances of a fraudulent quality or nature especially when several such **badges** occur at the same time or in the same situation.

Bad motive: Knowingly and willingly doing something wrongful.

Bail; bail bond: A signed agreement to ensure appearance in court or forfeit a cash penalty; it is a **cash bail bond** if a cash sum is posted as security and an **unsecured bail bond** if a signed agreement to pay the face amount upon failure to appear in court.

Bailiff: Uniformed officer of the court whose duty is to maintain order in the court during trial and to take custody of the jury and the defendant.

Ballistics (L., **ballista,** to hurl): Science of matching a fired bullet to the gun that fired it and gun and bullet characteristics and specifications.

Bankruptcy (L., **rupta,** to break): Financial insolvency with debts unpaid.

Bankruptcy Act: Federal law providing for the voluntary, involuntary or adjudged repossession and distribution of funds and property to satisfy creditors.

Bar (Middle English, **barre**): The legal profession; court or tribunal.

Barratry; barretry (Middle English, **barratrie,** to deceive): Inciting someone to frivolous litigation; stirring up controversy, conflict and quarrels through false rumors, exaggeration and delibeate provocation; deception.

Battery (L., **battuere,** to do battle, to beat): Unlawful physical force (**criminal battery**) or harmful treatment or unintentional injury such as professional services which exceed informed consent (**technical battery**). **Aggravated battery** involves violent injury, **simple battery** less violence.

Bench (Old English, **benc**): The court, judge, or judges in a court.

Bench trial: Trial by a judge only, without a jury.

Bench warrant: An order for arrest issued directly by a judge.

Bequeath (Old English, **becwethan,** to quote or say): to transfer personal property as a gift (**bequest**) in a **will**.

Best evidence; primary evidence: The most proven, objective evidence, original source documents; any lesser evidence is **secondary** such as copies of documents; **best evidence rule** is to require **original writing** except when such is not available.

Beyond a reasonable doubt: Standard of proof in criminal cases; the highest level of legal proof; to be entirely convinced, with 90 percent or more certainty of guilt or innocence.

Bifurcated trial: When there is more than one charge or issue in the same trial, such as damages and injury or wrongful death or criminal guilt and insanity.

Bill (L., **bulla,** seal): Has a variety of meanings: In **common law** a list of court costs (**bill of costs**), the trial transcript (**bill of evidence**), objections to the judge's handling of the case (**bill of exceptions**), statement of demands (**bill of particulars**). In **criminal law,** charges by a grand jury (**bill of indictment**) or by the prosecutor (**bill of particulars**), punitive legislation (**bill of attainder**). In **equity practice** there are **bills of certiorari, crossbills** (countersuits), **discovery, for a new trial, foreclosure, review** and **to take testimony.**

Binding instruction: When the judge **instructs the jury** as to the criteria for innocence or guilt to help them weigh the evidence and reach a **verdict.**

Bind over: When a court requires **bail** or **recognizance** that a defendant will appear in court as scheduled; also applies to referring a case to a higher court or **grand jury.**

Blue ribbon jury: A highly competent jury.

Boilerplate: Identical language or terms occurring in different documents; standard terminology, standard provisions.

Bona fide (L., **bona fidei,** good faith): Of, in and with good faith; honest, sincere, genuine, without fraud; **bad faith** is **mala fides;** unintentional mistakes are **bona fide errors.**

Borrowed servant; borrowed worker: Legal doctrine of a person who at a given time works under the direct supervision of another not normally that person's supervisor. A manager, foreman, worker, doctor, firefighter or police officer who directs someone in this way can be held liable for injury or damages rather than or in addition to the company, hospital, agency or department. Often used in medical malpractice to involve nurses, attendants and other hospital staff.

Boycott (19th century English, from **Charles C. Boycott**): An agreement, written, stated or tacit, to refuse to do business with an individual or firm; a shared conspiracy to restrict trade.

Brain death; brain dead: Statutory definition of death based on stopped brain function reflected in no response to reflex or stimulus, voluntary movement and a "flat" EEG recording for a 24-hour period; definition varies from state to state.

Breach (Old English, **bryce** or **brecan,** to break): Violation of law, duty, obligation, responsibility, standard or trust. **Breach of contract** is failure to fulfill a written, stated or implied contract; **breach of duty** is failure to provide services according to the current **state of the art** or **standards of care; breach of trust** is a wrongful omission or commission, willful or unintentional, of a duty or of **good faith** toward a beneficiary.

Breaking and entering; "b and e": Common Law burglary of **breaking** into and **entering** a place with intent to commit a **felony** (theft).

Bribery (Middle English, **bribe,** stolen): To offer, solicit, give or receive a reward in the form of money, property or preferential treatment; improper inducement or undue influence to effect favorable action.

Brief (L., **brevis,** summary): A formal, written summary of issues, evidence and witnesses to be presented at trial, filed in court.

Bring suit: Formal process of initiating and filing a legal proceeding (lawsuit).

Broad interpretation: Interpreting the overall intent, the general meaning or central principle of **constitutional** or **statutory law** rather than a focus on finer points or technicalities of a more literal interpretation.

Burden of persuasion; burden of proof: Criteria for or standard of evidential proof required in a case. (See also **Beyond a reasonable doubt: Clear and convincing; Preponderance of evidence.**)

But for test: Used in malpractice and negligence cases to determine whether there would have been injury or damages except for (**but for**) the defendant's actions.

By virtue of: Because of, by authority or reason of, **pursuant to.**

Calendar (L., **kalendarium,** loaner's account book): Listing of pending cases for trial; **calendar call** is a court session in which **cases are called** to determine their status and scheduling.

Calumny (L., **calumnia,** to deceive): To defame, wrongly or falsely accuse, to slander.

Camera; in camera (L., **camera,** chamber): The judge's **chamber** or office; held in the judge's office and/or not in open court (no spectators).

Capacity (L., **capacitas,** capability): Legal competence, legal responsibility, fitness; **criminal capacity** is the legal accountability or liability for one's actions. (See also **Competence.**)

Captain of the ship: Legal doctrine arising from the **borrowed servant** concept and usually applied in medical malpractice cases holding a doctor liable for the actions of others such as nurses, attendants and other staff.

Caption (L., **captus,** to take): The heading, like a newspaper headline, a brief descriptive statement of names of defendant and plaintiff, the court and case number.

Care (Old English, **caru,** to lament): Careful, watchful attention, diligent, conscientious concern. Key concept in **negligence** cases where **standard of care** requires **reasonable conduct** in direct proportion to risk of injury. **Slight care** is a standard based on common everyday situations by persons who are minimally **reasonable and prudent; reasonable, due** or **ordinary care** is a standard applied to what a **reasonable and prudent person** would provide in a situation similar to that of the defendant; **great care is provided by reasonable and prudent** persons in serious situations above and beyond the ordinary, requiring great caution, extra attention and effort; **highest degree of care** is the standard set by law and **standards of practice** in the field used by others than the defendant to provide service and protect the public.

Carnal (L., **carnalis,** of the flesh): Relating to the flesh in a sensual, sexual context. **Carnal knowledge** or **statutory rape** is sexual contact with full or partial penetration of the vagina. In some states sexual acts other than intercourse are included under this term. Elsewhere such limited but sexual contact is **carnal abuse.**

Case (L., **casus,** an event, an opportunity): Cause, conflict situation, lawsuit; criminal action investigated by police; physical or mental injury or disease treated by a physician or therapist; **agreed** or **stated case** is a written agreement of both sides to abide by a court's decision without trial; **case on appeal** is awaiting review on an **appelate court** docket; **case reserved** or **special case** is based on **points of law** which arose but could not be decided at the initial trial will be processed at another trial.

Cases and controversies: Term in the U. S. Constitution which sets the standard for court review to enforce rights and decide wrongs, requiring clarity and simplicity.

Case law: The body of data made up of actual court cases rather than laws and statutes which apply to them. (See also **Common law**.)

Cause (L., **causa,** the reason for): The precipitating event, cause, reason and basis for a legal proceeding (**cause of action**); **probable** or **reasonable cause** is when there is more evidence for than against, sufficient grounds to litigate; **proximate cause** is the precipitating action or lack of action causing injury without which no injury would occur; **for cause** is a term used when someone is removed from office for **legal cause,** not at the discretion of the appointing authority.

Caveat (L., **cavere,** beware): Warning by an **interested party** to avoid certain proscribed actions such as when an appeal is being taken; **caveat emptor** (buyer beware) is the legal doctrine that a purchaser is obligated to examine material before purchase.

Cease and desist: Administrative or court order forbidding a specified act or activity, such as deceptive advertising, misrepresentation, unfair labor practice, patent infringements.

Cede (L., **cedere,** to yield): Assign, transfer, grant, give, withdraw or surrender to, used mostly in land transactions.

Center of gravity: Legal doctrine that the court with the most direct contact with an event has jurisdiction; also known as **the most significant relationship theory.**

Certain; certainty (L., **certus,** decide, sift, discern): Precisely identified, defined, definite, without a doubt, mistake or ambiguity, from the evidence at hand.

Certificate (L., **certificatus,** to certify): Written confirmation that a specified act or action has been done or a law or standard satisfied, such as business or professional licenses, fire, building and safety permits; a **notary pulic** issues a **certificate of acknowledgment** when witnessing and dating voluntary signatures to documents; **certificate of need** is required to change occupancy of health facilities.

Certify (L., **certus,** to be certain): To attest in writing that something is true or as represented; **certified copy:** a copy of a document identified by signature of the person who has the original that the copy is authentic.

Certiorari, writ of (L., to inform of): An order by a higher court for the records of a lower court for the purpose of case review; used by U. S. Supreme Court to choose its cases and less frequently by state courts.

Challenge (L., **calumniari,** to falsely accuse): To object, take exception, dispute, confront, question or argue a right or qualification or the validity of evidence. **Challenge for cause** is a lawyer's request to disqualify a juror for a stated reason. There are a limited number of **peremptory challenges** allowed, the lawyer disqualifying a juror without need to explain the reason. Disputing the qualifications of the entire jury is a **challenge to the jury array.**

Chamber, judge's chamber (L., **camera,** chamber): The judge's office or private room.

Champion (L., **campio,** warrior): Advocate, defender, one who speaks for another, an attorney.

Chancery, courts of (Old French, **chancerie,** by chancellor): Courts of equity; the equity process. (See also **equity**.)

Change of venue (L., **venire,** to come): Removal of a suit from one court to another on the basis of fairness, convenience or jurisdiction. (See also **Extradition**.)

Character (Greek, **character,** mark or engrave): The totality of traits which make a personality distinctive, habit patterns and life-style, ethical values or moral predisposition, what you are in reality as opposed to **reputation,** what others see in you; **good character** is the total of positive attributes, **bad character** is the dark side of evil traits; **character witnesses** testify as to a person's **character.**

Characterization: Applying specific laws to the case in point; a lawyer painting a verbal picture (**characterizing**) to discount or discredit a person or organization or to improve the image of the lawyer's client.

Charge (L., **carrus,** a vehicle): An accusation, claim or contention (criminal law); duty or obligation, liability or lien (civil law). **Charge to the jury** is the judge's final remarks to the jury, explaining the rules of law that apply in the case and the verdict alternatives. **Public charge** is an ill or destitute person supported solely by public assistance funds.

Chattel (L., **capitale,** cattle): Personal property, animal or object, movable, not real estate.

Child abuse: Physical or psychological injury to a minor by molesting, striking, cruelty or negligence. (See also **Abuse; Assault; Battery;** and **Carnal knowledge**.)

Chilling effect: Legal doctrine in **constitutional law** to describe the deterrent or **chilling effect** of any law, act, action or practice that interferes with a **constitutional right** such as the right to vote, to appeal, free press, religious worship, etc.

Circuit court: Courts of general original jurisdiction based on a "circuit" of several counties or districts.

Circumstantial evidence: Evidence based on inference and not on eyewitness testimony; to infer from known facts what usually and reasonably can be expected to occur and establish the expectation as principal fact.

Citation, cite (L., **citare,** to move, set in motion): A court writ (summons) or police officer's order (traffic ticket) to appear in court on a specified data for a specified purpose or **show cause** why this is not done; to refer to legal precedents, articles, books, or briefs (**citation of authorities**).

Citizen's arrest: When a person who is not a law enforcement officer arrests another for a misdemeanor or felony witnessed or when there is **reasonable cause** to believe the person thus arrested committed the wrongful act.

Civil action; civil law: Legal proceedings and local laws which protect or enforce the rights of private citizens.

Civil commitment: A court order after a **commitment hearing** to confine a person judged to be a substance abuser or mentally ill or both and in need of treatment to a residential or inpatient treatment facility. A judge can issue a court order for civil commitment to prison for nonpayment of debts on the grounds the unpaid debts are in **contempt of court** or **civil contempt.**

Claim (L., **clamare,** to cry out): To assert and demand rights, such as the right to payment, property, privilege, and equitable settlement of breach of duty or performance.

Claims-made policy: In malpractice or similar insurance policies, the carrier (insurance company) covers only lawsuits filed during the term of the policy. An **occurrence policy** covers the insured for alleged malpractice which occurred during the term of the policy, even if the suit is filed years after the policy has lapsed.

Class action: A case where the plaintiff represents a clearly defined group or **class** of persons too numerous for all of them to appear in court, such as civil rights, product liability and antitrust cases.

Class of crime: The classification system describing crimes by type, seriousness, nature and appropriate punishments for each, such as **felony** (e.g. murder, grand theft) or **misdemeanor** (e.g. speeding ticket). There are degrees of severity (e.g. **murder in the first degree** or **Class B misdemeanor**).

Clear and convincing: Standard of proof in civil cases, between **Preponderance of evidence** and **Beyond a reasonable doubt,** and which is considered to be 75 percent certain, convincing, leaving little doubt.

Clear and present danger: Legal doctrine in **constitutional law** that the government can restrict freedom to protect the public in situations of great danger. Yelling "fire!" in a crowded theater is a simplistic example of how freedom of speech can endanger life and safety.

Clear title: A title free of liens, unencumbered, marketable.

Clemency: Mercy, compassion, leniency, as when a governor changes (**commutes**) a death sentence to life imprisonment.

Clerk (L., **clericus**): Officer of the court who files records and court papers, issues subpoenas and **swears-in** witnesses.

Client (L., **clinare,** to lean on): A person who confides in and contracts with an attorney for legal services.

Client's privilege: The confidentiality between client and attorney which prevents disclosure in court as specified by the client.

Closing argument: Attorney's final statement to the court summing up the case, the points proven and those not proven by opposing counsel.

Code, codify (L., **caudex, codex,** trunk of a tree or inscribed waxed wood tablet): An organized collection of laws with revisions. **Uniform Code of Military Justice** is the substantive and procedural law for all branches of the military service. The **Code of Professional Responsibility** is the ethical code of the American Bar Association which applies to all attorney members; it has been adopted by most states.

Codicil (L., **codicillus,** book): An addendum or supplement to a will which changes provisions of the will.

Coercion (L., **coercere,** to enclose): Direct or implied mental or physical threat, act or action which in effect compels someone to act against the will and free choice.

Cold blood: First-degree murder, planned and premeditated.

Collusion (L., **collusus,** secret pact): A hidden or secret agreement with intent to defraud or for mutual gain toward an unlawful goal; deceit, conspiracy, connivance.

Color, to give color (L., **celare,** to conceal): Expressed or implied, deceptive appearance, slanted, obscured, flavored, feigned, not real and usually of no substance, legally weak. An overstated, exaggerated claim is **a colorable cause;** an attempt to deceive or misrepresent is **a colorable transaction;** arbitrary use of power or law is **color of law.**

Commit (see **Civil commitment.**)

Common knowledge: Information a court accepts with proof, as self-evident, that which any **reasonable person** knows.

Common law: Legal processes and procedures based on custom, usage and tradition "of immemorial antiquity" and from legal precedents (**case law**) from England and the United States, excluding laws passed by legislature (**statutory law**).

Common law marriage: A mutual agreement to live together and assume marital duties and responsibilities but without a marriage license or wedding ceremony. Common-law marriages are not valid in about half the United States.

Community property: Property owned mutually by husband and wife, each with 50 percent interest (valid only in eight states). Most states are bound by **common law** which prescribes that husband and wife are entitled only what each has paid for.

Commutation (L., **commutatus,** back and forth): Change by substitution such as from death to a life sentence, payment by installment rather than in a lump sum, work for money or money for work.

Comparative negligence: Legal doctrine which assesses negligence by percentage, such as when both defendant and plaintiff are judged negligent in differing degrees, or when there are several defendants, or where the negligence is rated as to severity: **slight, ordinary,** or **gross.**

Compensation (L., **compensatus,** to equate): Payment equivalent to damages, injury, services rendered, fees or privileges; the monetary equivalent of injury, loss and for **pain and suffering.**

Competence; competency (L., **competere,** able, suitable): Legally qualified and fit to testify (**compos mentis**). To be **legally competent** to make a will, you must know what a will is, be aware of the property to be willed, the relationship of those included and omitted, and simple business transactions. To be **competent to stand trial** you must understand the charges against you. Court procedures and be able to consult with an attorney and assist in your own defense. A **competent witness** is one who is legally qualified to tesitfy. **Competent evidence is admissible (material** and **relevant**).

Complaint (L., **complangere,** to lament): The first step or initial pleading in a case. In **civil cases** it is a brief statement of the grounds and essential facts, damages sought and intention to go to trial. In **criminal cases** it is a charge that a crime has been committed, an offer to prove it and a request for trial to prosecute; if the magistrate agrees a **warrant** is issued.

Complicity (L., **complicare,** closely connected): The act of being a conspirator, accompliance or **accessory before the fact.**

Conclusion (L., **conclusio,** to end): Final statement in a plaintiff's complaint; closing argument or summation by attorneys at end of trial; **conclusion of fact** is a judgment on the validity of evidence; **conclusion of law** is statement of applicable law by the judge based on the jury's verdict or by the judge alone in a nonjury trial.

Concurrent sentences: When more than one sentence is counted as served during the same time interval; used in some cases when someone has been convicted for several crimes.

Confession (L., **confessus,** to confess): A voluntary statement admitting to the commission of crime; a **judicial confession** is one made in court, **extrajudicial confessions** are those made elsewhere. Confessions are further classified as **naked** if there is no external evidence, **indirect** if guilt is inferred by the defendant's conduct, **implied** if there is no confession but the defendant asks for the mercy of the court (i.e. a light sentence), **involuntary** if given under duress or some promise, **voluntary** if done of one's free will and accord.

Confidentiality (L., **confidere,** to trust): To be kept secret, held in confidence, not for public disclosure, such as between lawyer and client, doctor or therapist and patient, clergy and confessor. **Confidential communication** is made between two persons and of such quality as to be shared only by those two and no others. Court decisions in recent years have ruled confidentiality can and should be breached if there is a life-threatening emergency, clear and imminent danger to or by the client (**Tarasoff decision, California**).

Conflict of interest: Situations where persons in positions of trust (**fiduciary responsibility**) are exposed to opportunity for personal gain in the trust relationship.

Confrontation (L., **confrontare,** to bind): Sixth Amendment right to be faced by your accuser and which legally allows the defendant to cross-exaimine the witness.

Conjecture (L., **conjectura,** to throw together): Probable but not proven tentative conclusion, too weak to satisfy the rules of evidence; having some truth, an "educated guess" but surmise, supposition.

Consanguinity (L., **consanguineus,** with the blood): Blood relatives, common forbears, kin.

Conscience, right of: Freedom of conscience and free will, a constitutional right.

Consent (L., **consentire,** to sense or feel): A deliberate act of reason by a legally competent person to voluntarily choose what is offered in good faith by another; permission, accord, acquiescence, compliance, concurrence; **express consent** is direct, clear and unequivocal, written or verbal; **implied consent** is assumed by the nature of actions taken such as consenting to airport security checks, customs inspections, or highway traffic laws; **informed consent** is to freely choose or decline treatment or services based on adequate, understandable information by a reasonable and prudent practitioner as to expected effect, cost, time, risk and alternatives; in rape cases submission is not consent if the victim chooses to submit to avoid injury or death or resists until overcome.

Conservator (L., **conservare,** to keep): Court-appointed guardian, to manage the estate or affairs of a legally incompetent person or who liquidates a bankrupt business.

Consideration (L., **considerare,** to observe stars): Influence, enticement, inducement or motive to enter into a contract, such as for profit, reward, interest, right or ownership; as to time they are **concurrent, continuing** or **past**; by content they are **good, gratuitous, meritorious, moral, pecuniary, nominal, express, implied, sufficient, illegal** or **impossible.**

Conspiracy (L., **conspirare,** inhaling the same air together): Two or more persons joining together to jointly commit an unlawful act, or using unlawful means toward a lawful goal, or a lawful act which when done together is unlawful.

Conspiracy in restraint of trade is an unlawful agreement with intent to obstruct free trade or control the flow of trade (**Clayton and Sherman Antitrust Acts**).

Constitutional law: State and federal laws which describe the fundamental principles of government and law, their relationship to citizens, and provisions for legislature amendment, executive administration and judicial interpretation.

Consummation (L., **consummare,** to finish, to complete): To finish or complete; a marriage is **consummated** by sexual intercourse between the married partners.

Contempt of court: An act, by commission or omission, which interferes with a court, defies its authority or attacks its dignity; **direct** or **criminal contempt** is done directly in the courtroom or nearby, such as disobeying a command or order or acting out in court, is punishable by fine and/or prison; **indirect or constructive contempt** is not done in court (e.g. as refusal to obey a decree, injunction or order); **civil** or **quasi contempt** is disrespect to a party in court and not the court itself and is punishable by fine only.

Contentious (L., **contendere,** to contend): Litigated or contested between opposing parties; being antagonistic, belligerent, litigious.

Contingency contract; contingency fee: Agreed percentage of the amount of damages to be paid to an attorney as the legal fee rather than paying the attorney by the hour and for other costs of services rendered.

Continuance; continuance nisi: Postponement to another date, with a specified condition or for a prescribed period of time.

Contract (L., **contractus,** agreement): Usually a signed, dated written agreement to do something according to the terms specified. Health care providers should have written, dated and signed **treatment contracts** to document **informed consent,** but even without them there is an **implied contract** by the client receiving services. The contract is in force even if the client does not pay for services and continues until the provider documents notice of termination.

Contributory negligence (see **Negligence**).

Controlled substance: A drug listed in state or federal Controlled Substances Acts.

Convey; conveyance (L., **conviare,** away from): To transfer title or property to another; the legal instrument used to effect the transfer is the **conveyance.**

Conviction (L., **convictus**): Final result of effect of criminal trial proceedings (**guilty** or **nolo contendere**).

Convincing proof: Sufficient proof to convince an unprejudiced mind. (See also **Beyond a reasonable doubt; Clear and convincing; Preponderance.**)

Coroner's inquest: Jury review held by the coroner as to the cause of death if by violence or under suspicious circumstances.

Corpus delicti (L., dead body): The human or material remains upon which a crime was committed (i.e. a person, building or object).

Corpus juris (L., body of law): Lawbooks or collections of law such as the **Corpus Juris Secundum,** a compendium of American law, the **Corpus Juris Civilis** based on Roman Law or **Corpus Juris Canonici** based on ecclesiastical or "canon law" of the Roman Catholic Church.

Corroborate (L., **corroboratus,** strength): To make credible, confirm, strengthen, add weight to, such as when testimony is validated by other facts or testimony.

Corroborating evidence: Evidence which augments or supplements that already given and which substantiates and confirms it.

Costs; court costs: Defendant and plaintiff expenses not including attorney's fees.

Counsel (L., **consilium,** to consult): Attorney; legal advice; also to **aid and abet** a felon to commit a crime.

Counsellor: Attorney.

Counsel of record: Attorney who files legal papers and is listed in them as legal representative of a client in the case.

Counsel, right to: Sixth and Fourteenth Amendment constitutional right of a criminal defendant to be represented by an attorney in legal proceedings if unable to pay for them.

Count (L., **computare,** to consider): A ground for action, part of a criminal indictment, part of a declaration or statement, separate, independent claim.

Counterclaim: Opposing claim of a defendant in response to the plaintiff's initial claim.

Countermand: To revoke an express or implied order, instruction or authority.

Countersuit: Suit filed by defendant against plaintiff or the plaintiff's attorney.

Court calendar: Listing of pending pretrial, motions, trial or appeal proceedings.

Court-martial: A military court to process charges against members of the military service under the Uniform Code of Military Justice (UCMJ). Can be **general, special or summary** depending on seriousness.

Court of Admiralty: Federal district court action specific to maritime law.

Court of Appeals: State or federal courts which "hear" appeals from defendants who lost lower court decision and who seek to have that initial decision reversed.

Court of Bankruptcy: Federal court with specific jurisdiction over the formal legal process of bankruptcy.

Court of Chancery; Court of equity: Courts which process equity cases as opposed to a court of law or common law, although where **Rule of Civil Procedure** prevail all these types of cases are merged into the common category of **civil actions.**

Court of Law: State or federal court; usually used to differentiate the court from a court of chancery or equity.

Court of Military Appeals: Federal appelate criminal court which reviews court-martial convictions from all military services. Interestingly, there are three civilian judges appointed by the President of the United States.

Court of Nisi Prius: Now used to identify a civil trial court but originally applied only to a Philadelphia court over which only a state supreme court judge presided.

Court reporter: Officer of the court who transcribes court proceedings and/or who publishes court decisions.

Courts of Record: Courts with the legal authority to fine or imprison for contempt and whose proceedings are permanently recorded and thus "of record."

Covenant (L., **convenire,** to agree): Promise, agreement or contract, verbal or written, between parties to agree to do or not do something or which states a shared truth, cause or value.

Covert (Middle English or Middle French, to cover or conceal): Sheltered, concealed, protected, covered, not openly apparent.

Credentials (L., **credere,** to believe or trust): Documentary evidence of a person's qualifications and/or authority.

Credibility (L., **credere,** to believe or trust): Worthy of belief. **Competence** must always be established before credibility can be considered.

Credibly informed: Used in legal documents to differentiate an opinion based on authentic, trustworthy secondary sources (documents, statements of others) and not personal firsthand experience.

Creditor (L., **creditum,** what is owed to another): One to whom money or some legal consideration is owed.

Crime (L., **crimen,** fault, accusation): A serious violation of state or federal law, by omission or commission, punishable by fine, imprisonment or loss of office or title. Examples of crimes of commission are assault, murder, and robbery; crimes of omission involve a breach or failure to act such as manslaughter, negligence, and abandonment. (See also **Felony** and **Misdemeanor**.)

Criminal (L., **criminalis**). Pertaining to crime, to the perpetrator and also to the legal and judicial process for trial and conviction (**criminal procedure** or **proceedings**).

Criminal insanity: Due to mental disease or defect (mental illness) unable to know right from wrong and/or conform conduct to what is right and avoid doing what is wrong.

Criminal justice system: The formal, organized system of courts and procedures to try and convict criminals.

Criminal law: Law which specifies and defines what are crimes, punishment for their violation, and legal proceedings used to process them from arrest to trial and conviction or acquittal.

Criminology: The science of crime, punishment, rehabilitation and prevention.

Critical stage: In criminal proceedings, any point at which the defendant should have access to an attorney and without which rights are lost, defenses and privileges waived, or the effect would be prejudicial presently or in the future.

Cross-action: Defendant's counterclaim or countersuit against the plaintiff in the same case.

Cross-appeal: A plaintiff's appeal against an appellant defendant.

Cross-claim (see **Cross-action**).

Cross-complaint (see **Cross-action).**

Cross-examination: Examination of a witness by the opposing attorney, at deposition or during trial.

Cross-interrogatory: Cross-questions or a list of questions submitted by a party which has previously been served with interrogatories.

Cruel and inhuman treatment: Unwarranted and unjustified conduct causing suffering and/or distress, making life unbearable and destroying peace of mind. Most used in divorce cases.

Cruel and unusual punishment: Treatment which a reasonable person would find unfair, undignified, offensive, insensitive or shocking; unnecessary, excessive force; specifically prohibited by the Eighth Amendment.

Cruelty (L., **crudelis,** to act cruelly): Intentional, malicious inflicting of mental or physical suffering.

Culpability (L., **culpa,** guilt): Liable, deserving blame. Criminal culpability requires legal proof that the defendant acted knowingly, willingly and/or negligently or recklessly to every material element of the offense(s).

Cumulative sentence; Separate, additional sentences imposed for different offenses against the same convicted felon.

Custody (L., **custodia,** guarding): Safekeeping, preservation, within the direct and immediate care of a designated person or party, not final title. Can apply to a person or an object. **Custodia legis** or **custody of the law** applies to repossession under a writ by a court or public officer.

Custom and usage: A practice which by long-standing time and custom has acquired the force of law. **Custom** refers to the same situation which has been resolved the same way, and **usage** refers to a repetition of the same acts (or customs).

Dactylography: The scientific study of fingerprints.

Damages: Loss or injury to a person, property or rights expressed in monetary terms, caused by the actions or lack of action of another.

Damage is the loss or injury; **damages** is that loss or injury expressed in terms of financial compensation. **Actual damages** are real actual damages and the amount awarded for them; **compensatory damages** pay only for the injury and no more; **criminal damage** is willful damage or destruction of property; **exemplary or punitive damages** are over and above actual and compensatory, to "make an example of" and punish the defendant; **nominal damages** are a trifling amount (like one dollar) acknowledging technical liability or where the plaintiff does not establish extent or worth of damage.

Danger invites rescue: Liability of a person creating a dangerous situation or condition for another, but a third person attempts rescue and is injured.

Danger to self or others: In civil commitment hearings, a necessary ground to establish mental illness in need of treatment. **Danger to self** is an inability to care for one's self such as eating, confusion or wandering; **danger to others** is putting others in **clear and immediate or imminent danger** of injury or death.

Dangerous weapon: An object or instrument which by its malicious use can or did cause injury or death.

Deadlocked jury: A jury unable to reach the required unanimous decision or **verdict.** Also known as a **hung jury.**

Death: The terminal or permanent cessation of vital signs and organ functions. (See also **Brain death.**)

De bene esse: Conditionally or provisionally, anticipating a future challenge. **Examination de bene esse** is a pretrial deposition of a witness who may not be available for trial used at trial if the witness is not present.

Decedent (L., **decedere,** to depart, die): A recently deceased person. **Decedent's estate** is property, real and personal, in possession at time of death, title transferring to the heirs upon death subject to **last will and testament** and any probate court requirements. **Intestate** means without a will; **testate** applies to one who dies leaving a will.

Decision (L., **decidere,** to decide): Determination resulting from due process review and consideration of the facts of law.

Declaration (L., **declarare,** to make clear): In common law, the plaintiff's first pleading or formal exposition of the case consisting of title, venue, commencement, cause, counts and conclusion. It is a **petition** in civil law, a **complaint** in federal courts and states under the Federal Rules of Civil Procedure.

Declaratory judgment: A judgment which declares rights and status of the contesting parties or the opinion of the court without ordering any action or settlement.

Declaratory statute: Declares the meaning and intent of a previous statute, to clarify it and settle controversy regarding it.

Decree (L., **decernere,** to sift, decide). The judgment of a court; **final decree** is the ultimate disposition of a case; **interlocutory decree** is preliminary, not final.

Deep pockets: Refers to filing suit against any and all parties involved directly or even indirectly to ensure sufficient assets or insurance coverage to pay damages if the suit is successful.

De facto (L., in actual fact). What is accepted for practical purposes but is technically not legitimate; reality vs. theoretical or fact vs. formalities. A **de facto** official is in office but may not have a clear legal right to be there (e.g. dictators, military governor); a **de facto** marriage is of questionable legality. **De Jure** is the opposite, meaning legal, proper just.

Defamation (L., **diffamare,** to harm, disgrace). Injury to a party's reputation, dignity of esteem verbally (**slander**) or in writing (**libel**) exposing the injured party to ridicule, hatred and adverse opinion.

Default (L., **defallere,** to fail): When a defendant fails to appear for trial or does not plead within the time limit.

Defect (L., **defectus,** lack or failing): A deficiency or absence of something essential; can be **latent** (not readily apparent), **fatal** (nullifying a contract), **patent** (normally evident); **mental** (mental illness).

Defendant (L., **defendere,** to strike): The person or party sued (civil cases) or charged with a crime (criminal cases).

Defense: The evidence and arguments against the plaintiff in civil cases or the prosecutor in criminal cases. Can be **affirmative** if based on new facts; **frivolous** if insufficient or pretentious; **legal** if complete and adequate; **meritorious** if on essential points of law; **peremptory** if charging the plaintiff's case is not legal. (See also **Insanity defense**.)

Defer (L., **differe,** to postpone): Delay, remand, postpone but not to abolish.

Deferred sentence: When sentencing is postponed to another date and time.

Definitive (L., **definitus,** delimited): Final conclusion or end such as **definitive judgment.**

Defraud (L., **defraudare,** to cheat): To knowingly or recklessly misrepresent a material.

Degree (L., **degradus,** step or stage): Extent, measure or stage such as **degrees** of **proof** (see **proof**), **crime** (first- or second-degree murder, felony v. misdemeanor), **kin** (between deceased and descent of heirs), **negligence** (ordinary v. gross).

De jure (see **De facto**).

Deliberate (L., **deliberare,** to weigh, ponder): To examine, review, consider, weigh, ponder as to strengths and weaknesses, for and against.

Delict (L., **delictum,** a wrong): Wrongful acts and inadvertent injury, from Roman law and more broadly defined than **tort.**

Demand (L., **demandare,** to mandate): Claim or charge; summons to appear in court; asserting a legal right; a called debt.

Demeanor: Observed behavior and physical appearance. **Demeanor evidence** is a witness's behavior on the stand which can be considered by the court to lessen credibility.

Demonstrate (L., **demonstrare,** to show): To prove, satisfy legal proof by evidence and reasoning.

Demur; demurrer (L., **demorari,** to linger): To formally take exception, usually when defendant admits factual truth of complaint or answer but claims they are insufficient for reasons stated. It is a **demurrere to evidence** if it challenges opponent's evidence; **demurrer to interrogatories** if objecting to an interrogatory especially at deposition.

Denial (L., **denegare,** to negate): Challenging, negating opponent's entire case (**general denial**) or any part of it (**specific denial**).

De novo (L., new): Fresh, new, another or second time. When a case is retried it is called a **trial de novo.**

Dependent (Middle French, **dependre,** hanging from): One who largely or solely relies on or is supported by another.

Deponent (L., **deponere,** to put): A witness who gives testimony under oath which is then written, or swears to the truth of a written statement.

Deposition: A witness's sworn verbal or written pretrial testimony to questions by opposing attorney who can cross-examine; part of **discovery process** and not done in court.

Depraved mind: Highest degree of malice, an inherent defect of morality and rectitude rendering someone indifferent to the life of others; spite, hate, evil mind, ill will. Also known as **depravity of heart.**

Detainer (L., **detinere,** to detain): The act or fact of legally or illegally withholding property or a person's liberty (**detention**).

Detention hearing: Proceeding to determine whether or not a person should be detained against his/her will.

Determinate sentence: Sentence for a fixed (**determinate**) time. An **indeterminate sentence** is not fixed and depends in part on the prisoner's behavior which can shorten the sentence.

Determination (L., **determinare,** to set limits): A court or administrative decision or finding; when a right, power or interest ends; a judgment or conclusion after review.

Devise (L., **divisus,** divide): Disposing of real or personal property by a **last will and testament** of the deceased to another. The recipient is the **devisee.**

Dicta; dictum (L., **dictus,** opinion): Judge's opinion in the case at hand, not binding in other cases, made without argument or full consideration of it and not necessarily the judge's final conclusion or opinion on the matter.

Digest (L., **digestus,** orderly collection): Compendium or compilation of court cases or other materials arranged alphabetically by title; an index of titles and abstracts.

Dijudication: Judicial determination or decision.

Dilatory defense: Challenge or defense to dismiss or delay a suit without discussing merits of the case until the obstacle is removed.

Diligence (L., **diligentia,** haste, speed): Attentive care; continuing, conscientious activity; in civil law can be **slight, ordinary** or **extraordinary.** (See also **Care.**)

Diligent inquiry: An inquiry a diligent man would make, in good faith and fitting to the situation and circumstances.

Diminished capacity: Legal doctrine referring to the state of mind necessary to be legally liable to commit a crime, and if proved has the effect of reducing sentencing. (See also **Insanity; Mental disease; Defect**).

Direct attack: Proceeding (injunction, writ of error, appeal, bill of review) to stop some act or judgment.

Directed verdict: Judge's instruction to the jury to arrive at a specific verdict; a judge rendering a decision when there are insufficient grounds or evidence to warrant the trial process.

Direct evidence: Firsthand eyewitness testimony or primary source documents.

Direct examination: First interrogation of a witness by the attorney requesting that testimony; precedes cross-examination by opposing attorney.

Disability: Inability or incapacity to fully enjoy legal rights and/or gainful employment due to age, physical or mental state or incarceration (in prison). Classified as **general** or **special, personal** or **absolute, civil** or **physical,** and **partial, temporary, permanent** or **total.**

Disavow: To reject, repudiate, deny the actions and right to authority of an agent.

Disbarment: Court action to revoke or suspend an attorney's license to practice.

Disclaimer: To reject and refuse the authority of or a claim by a person or of an interest, right or property.

Disclosure: Act of releasing or imparting information such as **Truth in Lending Act, Freedom of Information Act,** and product specifications under patent laws. (See also **Discovery**.)

Discontinuance: Ending litigation, dismissal.

Discovered peril doctrine: Legal doctrine that there is a moral duty to avoid injuring others. The doctrine has three parts: Plaintiff negligence created the dangerous situation; defendant discovered the peril in time to avoid injury using reasonable care for personal safety; failure to continue to exercise that care and safety.

Discovery; discoverability: The pretrial acquisition of knowledge from opposing side not previously available; obtained through interrogatories, depositions, private investigation, inspection and examination of evidence.

Discovery rule: In medical malpractice, cause of action begins when patient knew or should have known of the negligence of the practitioner.

Discredit: To destroy, impeach or diminish credibility of a witness and/or testimony or documentary evidence.

Discretionary acts: Judge or administrator's discretionary action based on facts and law, just and proper and not arbitrary or capricious.

Discretionary damages: Damages awarded at the discretion of an impartial jury considered as assessed by their enlightened consciences.

Discrimination: A legal doctrine from constitutional law, the effect of a practice or statute which excludes privilege from a class of persons and/or bestows special privilege on a class or persons arbitrarily or without reasonable distinction between classes involved; unfair practices; denial of privileges because of age, race, nationality or religion.

Dismissal without prejudice; Plaintiff can sue again on the same claim or cause of action; **dismissal with prejudice** forbids bringing suit again on the same claim or cause.

Dissent (L., **dissentire,** to feel, to sense): Disagreement usually of one judge with another or others.

Domicile (L., **domicillium,** dwelling): True, permanent home where you live. You can have several residences but only one **domicile.**

Double jeopardy: Legal doctrine based on constitutional and also common law prohibiting being prosecuted more than once for the same offense.

Draconian: Cruel, harsh, severe; taken from Draco, an Athenian lawgiver (c. 621 BC) who prescribed the death sentence for most offenses.

Due process (L., **debere,** debt; **processus,** progress): Legal procedures or **process** protecting the rights of both sides of a fair trial by an impartial judge or jury **due** them by their constitutional right; the regular course of law through the legal and judicial systems.

Embezzlement (Middle French, **enbesillier,** to destroy): Illegal and fraudulent misuse of money or property.

Enjoin (L., **injungere,** to join): Court order to do or not do whatever is specified by the order.

Entrapment (middle French, **entraper,** to trap): When agents or officers entice or induce a person to commit a crime not actually planned by him/her for the ultimate purpose of prosecuting for it.

Equitable action: Legal action to prevent the threatened inflicting of injury or wrong.

Equity, Court of: Court which decides cases involving remedial justice, also known as **courts of chancery.**

Escheat (L., **excadere,** to fall): The right of the state to claim and acquire an estate when there is no other legally clear or valid claim to it.

Escrow (Middle French, **escroue,** a scroll): Funds or documents held by a designated third person until some contingency or condition has been satisifed.

Estoppel (Middle French, **estouper,** a bung or stopper): A person's acts or acceptance of certain facts or conditions which prevents later making claim to challenge them.

Et al. (L., **et alii**): Means "and others." Smith et al. means Smith and others.

Et seq. (L., **et sequentes**): Means "and the following." Used to refer to statutes such as Section 42 et seq. meaning Section 42 and what follows in that section.

Exception: A verbalized formal objection by an attorney during trial proceedings which refuses or seeks to overrule an objection, implying s/he will seek reversal by appeal.

Ex contractu (L., out of contract): Rights and causes which arise from breach of contract.

Ex delicto (L., from a fault): Rights and causes arising from a wrong or **tort.**

Exhibit (L., **exhibibere,** to give): Document or object submitted as proof of facts or related to a subject or issue in court during trial or appeal, at hearings, or to agency officials, auditors, etc.

Ex parte (L., by or for a party): Done on behalf of a specified party and no one else.

Expert evidence: Technical, scientific or professional information given in sworn testimony by an **expert witness** qualified to speak authoritatively by reason of specialized knowledge, skill, training or experience, nominated by a litigant and qualified by the court.

Ex post facto (L., after the fact): A resultant act or fact which followed a previous act or fact and is related to it; the resulting realities from preceding events.

Extenuating circumstances: Mitigating or mediating factors which lessen the severity of a crime and which, if proved, lessen the severity of punishment.

Fair preponderance: In civil cases, sufficient evidence to satisfy the trier of fact that the **burden of proof** is met.

Felony (L., **fello,** evildoer): A serious crime, punishable by death or imprisonment. (See also **Misdemeanor; Crime.**)

Fiduciary (L., **fidere,** to trust): The good faith relationship legally binding on a person who functions as trustee for another (from Roman law).

Forgery (L., **fabrica,** to fashion): Intentional alteration of a written document to misrepresent or defraud.

Fraud (L., **fraus,** injury): Intentional distortion of facts to injure or cheat another of money or goods. (See also **defraud.**)

Garnish (Middle French, **garnir,** to warn): Legal claim to goods or money resulting form **garnishment proceedings.**

General demurrer: A **demurrer** questioning the validity of the basis of a claim.

Grand jury: A jury summoned to receive complaints and accusations of crime, hear and review evidence presented by the state, and issue indictments if satisified a crime has been committed. It's called **grand** because it's usually larger than usual, in common law ranging from 12 to 23.

Gratuitous guest: A passenger riding at the invitation of the owner or her/his agent and who does not pay a fare.

Guardian ad litem: Court-appointed **guardian** to look after the best interests of a minor or legally incompetent person.

Habeas corpus (Middle Latin, you should have the body): Taken from the first words of the old writ in Roman law. Refers to legal doctrine that when a person is detained s/he must be produced so the court can ensure no rights have been denied without due process of law.

Harmless error: An error found in a lower court by appelate review but not considered serious enough to reverse the lower court decision.

Hearsay: Testimony or evidence not based on a witness's own firsthand observation (e.g. relying on another's description, what was read not personally or professionally known or seen). Some attorneys try to discredit expert witness use of publications and references as hearsay.

Holographic will: A will (testamentary instrument) which is handwritten, dated and signed by a person (testator).

Hostile witness: A witness whose testimony is contrary to or which contradicts the side requesting that testimony. It subjects the witness to cross-examination by the side who requested the testimony, since it is inconsistent and antagonistic to that side.

Impeachment of witness: An attack on the credibility of a witness.

Inadmissible evidence: Not acceptable under the established rules of evidence.

In camera (L., in a chamber): Applies to proceedings held in the judge's office (chambers) or in court when the public has been excluded.

Incompetent evidence (See Inadmissible evidence).

Indeterminate sentence: A sentence which is indefinite, usually reading "not less than" and "not more than" so that the prisoner's attitude and behavior can lessen the actual time spent but within the specified range.

Indictment (Old French, **enditer,** to write down): The written finding of a grand jury that in their opinion a crime has been committed by the person specified.

Inferior court: A court which is "lower" than, subservient to a "higher" appelate court.

Injunction (L., **injunctus,** to enjoin): A writ of a court which prohibits a specified act(s).

Insanity (See **Mental disease or defect**).

Instruction (L., **instructus,** to build): Direction given by the judge to the jury pertaining to the points of law and due process and procedural requirements of the case.

Inter alia (L., and also): Means "among other things" or "and in addition" or "and also."

Inter alios (L., and between): Means "among these other persons" or "between these persons."

Interlocutory: Temporary, provisional, not final.

Interrogatory; interrogatories (L., **interrogare,** to ask): Written questions posed by one adversary to another, to be answered in writing under oath.

Intervention (L., **intervenere,** to come between): When a third party is permitted by the court to be involved in a suit. (See also **Amicus curiae.**)

Intestate (L., **intestatus,** without testate or will): A person who dies without leaving a last will and testament.

Irrelevant: Evidence which is not directly related or sufficiently related to the case or matter at issue.

Jurisprudence (L., **juris,** to judge; **prudens,** prudently): Both the science of law in its statutes and procedures and the philosophy of law in its theories and principles.

Jury (L., **jurare,** to swear): A designated number of citizens selected by specified legal procedure, sworn to impartially review evidence and determine and declare matters of fact by their verdict. A **petit jury** is the usual jury of twelve or less in civil and criminal trials. (See also **Dedlocked jury; Grand jury.**)

Leading questions: A question with implied direction which "leads" the witness toward a conclusion which supports the argument of the attorney asking the question. Leading questions are prohibited during **direct examination.** (See also **Cross-examination.**)

Letters rogatory (L., **rogare,** to ask): A letter from one court to another requesting that a witness residing in the other court's jurisdiction answer written questions which are enclosed with the letter.

Levy (Old French, **levee,** to raise): Obtaining money due and payable by the seizure and sale of property.

Liable (L., **ligare,** to bind up): In civil cases, the defendant's adjudged responsibility on the trial matters and issues. It is analogous to "guilty" in a criminal case.

Libel (L., **libellus,** in leaf or book): Defamatory print (i.e. writing, pictures, photos, signs, posters) which injures the reputation or impugns the character of another.

Lis pendens (L., law pending): Litigation which is still open, pending or currently in progress.

Locus delicti (L., locus or place of injury): Where an injury or offense occurred.

Malfeasance (French, **mal** ill, **feasance** doing): Committing a wrongful or illegal act.

Malicious prosecution: When a defendant is prosecuted without probable cause, inappropriately with intent to injure.

Mandamus (L., we enjoin you): A legal "do it" order (**writ of mandamus**) from a superior court to an inferior court to take some specified action.

Mandate: Court order to enforce the sentence or judgment of a decree.

Manslaughter: Taking the life of another but without malice or planning (aforethought: premeditation). It is **involuntary manslaughter** if it occurred incidental to commission of a crime and **voluntary manslaughter** if done by sudden or irresistible impulse.

Materiality; material evidence: Directly relating to the points of law and underlying substantive issues.

Mens rea (L., guilty mind): Criminal intent, a mind with guilty knowledge, wrongful purpose, evil intent.

Mental anguish: Pain, fear, anxiety, distress and similar resulting from physical or mental injury or loss; as indignation, shame, humiliation, frustration, etc. is grounds for divorce in some states.

Mental cruelty: Pattern of behavior of one spouse to the other to the degree as to be damaging to mental or physical health and making the marriage relaionship intolerable.

Mental disease or defect: Like **insanity** these are legal terms rather than medical or psychiatric, used to satisfy the requirements in civil law for commitment to a mental hospital and to make a will and in criminal law to determine competence to stand trial and criminal responsibility at the time of the offense. In most states, commitment criteria is danger to self or others, unable to care for self and suffering mental illness in need of inpatient treatment. To make a will, the person must understand what property is owned, the nature of a will, and the persons who will be recipients. For competence to stand trial, the defendant must understand the charges, trial process and how to cooperate with an attorney. Mental status at time of offense is determined by a detailed study of defendant's behaviors before and after the alleged crime. American Law Institute (ALI) Model Penal Code defines the **insanity defense** as proof of "mental disease or defect" which causes "lack of substantial capacity either to appreciate the criminality (wrongfulness) of his conduct or to conform his conduct to the requirements of law."

Mental suffering (See **Mental anguish** and **Mental cruelty).**

Misdemeanor: A minor criminal offense, less severe than a **felony,** and with lesser punishment (fine or shorter sentence served in a local jail, prison farm, community service, etc.).

Misfeasance: Improper performance of a lawful duty or act.

Mistrial: A trial which is not valid and therefore non-binding, due to improper procedure or inappropriate jurisdiction.

Mitigating circumstance: Circumstances which lessen the degree of moral culpability of an offense but do not justify the offense.

Moot (old English, **mote,** meet): Without clear precedent; undecided, unsettled.

Moral terpitude: Behavior which is contrary to societal values and standards, modesty or morality.

Motions: Written or oral requests by attorneys to the court before (**to dismiss**), during (**for directed verdict**), or after trial (**for new trial**). They are **ex parte** if given without notice.

Municipal courts: Courts established with jurisdiction specific to a city or community.

Murder (L., **morte,** death): Unlawful killing of a person (or fetus) with express or implied malice aforethought. It is **criminal homicide** when committed intentionally and knowingly or recklessly and with indifference such as during commission of another crime (e.g. rape, robbery, burglary or during an escape). In most states, **murder in the first degree** involves planning or extreme atrocity (sometimes called **mayhem, depraved heart murder**). **Second-degree murder** is usually "everything else." Some states have a third degree of murder.

Ne exeat (L., don't leave): A writ forbidding a designated person from leaving the jurisdiction of the court.

Negligence (L., **negligere,** to neglect): Failure to do what a reasonable and prudent person with ordinary considerations in a similar situation would or would not do. There are a variety of types, some of which are: **actionable,** when lack of due care was proximate cause of damage or injury; **contributory,** where the plaintiff's lack of care added to the defendant's; **criminal,** when life is endangered; **gross** if large scale reckless disregard.

Next friend: term used to describe a person who acts for a minor or other but who is not a court-appointed guardian.

Nisi prius courts (L., unless): Term used for courts held to try issues of fact before a judge or a judge and jury.

No bill: Term used by grand jury to indicate insufficient grounds or evidence for indictment.

Nol pros or **nolle prosequi** (L., no further prosecution): Formal entry by the plaintiff (or prosecutor) on the record stating there will be no further action taken on the case.

Nolo contendere (L., no contest): Criminal court plea by which the defendant neither admits nor denies charges but will accept fine or sentence; used in antitrust actions to prevent civil actions involving the same acts.

Nominal party: A party named in a suit only because technically required.

Non compos mentis (L., Unsound mind): Legally insane. Can mean mental illness or mental retardation according to current diagnostic criteria. (See also **Mental disease or defect**.)

Objection: Act of making known to the court a challenge to a statement or procedure. It is important that objections appear in the record in the event an appeal is filed.

Occurrence policy: A type of malpractice liability in which claims are covered during the period the policy was in effect, regardless of when they are filed **Claims-made policy** is one which applies to claims filed only when the policy is in effect, not afterward.

Of counsel: Term used to describe attorneys helping with a case but who are not the attorney of record.

Opening statement: The initial outline or summary of the case when trial begins with anticipated proof of points of law to be presented.

Opinion evidence: Testimony in the form of a witness's opinion such as by an **expert witness.** (See also **Expert evidence**.)

Ordinary: As used in law, normal, reasonable, regular, common, usual, customary. (See also **Care; Negligence**.)

Pain and suffering: Physical discomfort and/or mental distress claimed as recoverable damages.

Parties: Adversaries in litigation or principals in contracts and agreements.

Patient privilege: A patient's right of access to his or her records of treatment.

Peremptory challenge: The procedure used by an attorney to reject a prospective juror without explaining the reason for doing so. There are a designated number of such challenges available to attorneys on both sides.

Perjury (L., **perjurare,** to destroy): The crime of lying under oath; making a formal verbal or written statement known to be false. **Subornation of perjury** is inducing another to commit perjury.

Petition (L., **petitus,** a request): A formal written request for judicial action, to right a wrong, grant a favor, right, privilege or license. It is a First Amendment right.

Plaintiff (Middle French, **plaintif,** one who grieves): The party or person who complains or sues in a civil case: claimant.

Plea; pleading (L., **placere,** to be decided): Defendant's answer to plaintiff's declaration; **pleadings** are the formal allegations by advesaries of their claims and arguments.

Plea bargaining: In criminal cases where the prosecutor and defendant negotiate a mutually satisfactory disposition of the case which is then submitted to the court for approval.

Polling the jury: Asking each juror whether he or she agreed with the verdict.

Power of attorney: Written document authorizing another person to act as agent or attorney.

Praecipe (L., to instruct, be preceptor): Writ commanding the defendant to do what is specified; request to court clerk to issue summonses.

Precedent (L., **praecedere,** preceding): Prior similar cases used as illustrative examples and guides for the present case.

Prejudice (L., **proejudicium,** previous damage): Bias, preconceived opinion. (See also **Average person test** and **Dismissal without prejudice.**) **Prejudicial error** is when an appelate court finds sufficient prejudice in lower court proceedings to reverse the lower court's decision (also called **reversible error**).

Preponderance of evidence: Test of proof needed for a plaintiff to win a civil case, evidence which is greater in weight and more convincing than that placed against it, better than 50 percent certain.

Presumption (L., **praesumptus,** assumption): Rule of law which states that a finding that a fact is true based on inference from other laws or facts stands as true until it is refuted.

Prima facie (L., at first sight, on sight): Assumed to be true without evidence to the contrary.

Privilege (L., **privus,** private): A right or exemption beyond the law. **Privileged communication** is that confidential relationship of attorney-client, doctor-patient or priest-confessor. Breach of confidentiality can be grounds for suit. Privilege can be overcome by court order or to save a life.

Probable cause (See **Cause.**)

Probate: The act of processing a last will and testament.

Proof (L., **probare,** to prove): Establishing the level of belief required in the mind of triers of fact. In criminal cases the **standard of proof** is **beyond a reasonable doubt** (more than 90 percent certain). In civil cases, proof is **clear and convincing** (75 percent certainty) or **simple preponderance** (more than 50 percent certain); (see these terms elsewhere in this Glossary).

Prosecutor (L., **prosecutus,** to pursue): Attorney for the state or federal government in criminal case.

Proximate cause: In negligence cases, it must be proven that the plaintiff's injuries or damages were **directly** caused by the action or inaction of the defendant. (See **Cause.**)

Punitive damages (See **Damages**).

Quash (L., **cassus,** void): To void, annul, vacate or overcome, such as a summons or an indictment.

Quasi-judicial: The function of public administrative officers when they hear testimony, gather, review and analyze data, to ascertain facts, draw conclusions and decide disposition.

Question: In law, a disputed point to be debated, subject for investigation, to be decided by judge or jury. Types: **categorical** requiring a "yes" or "no" reply; **leading** or **hypothetical** as used in cross-examination; of **fact** or **law** depending on needs of the case.

Quid pro quo (L., what for what): A legal transaction in which something is exchanged for something else; mutual exchange of parties to a contract or agreement.

Quotient verdict: When each juror writes down the sum of damages s/he feels is warranted. Amounts for all jurors are added together then divided by the number of jurors. The resulting sum is the jury's verdict of damages.

Reasonable doubt: A legal doctrine which states that to justify acquittal doubt must arise from evidence or lack of it and be similar to that of a reasonable or prudent person.

Rebut; rebuttal: To refute statements made and evidence introduced; stage of trial when such rebuttal is appropriate.

Redirect examination: Conducted by attorney who originally requested the testimony; follows cross-examination.

Referee (L., **referre,** to bear): Court-appointed intermediary and therefore an officer of the court to take testimony and report back to the court.

Refreshing the memory: The act of a witness checking back into documents to "refresh memory" of details related to testimony.

Release: To relinquish a right, privilege or claim; discharge of a debt; plaintiff's signed agreement to accept awarded damages as final.

Relevant; relevancy: Bearing, applicability; when one fact validates another or makes either or both facts more probable; **materiality** refers to evidence clearly and directly connected with trial issues.

Reply: The plaintiff's argument responding to the defendant's initial **answer** to the plaintiff's claim.

Res ipsa iquito (L., it speaks for itself): When damages or injury is an obvious result of negligence.

Res judicata (L., it is judged): Legal precedents to the present case.

Respondeat superior (L., Let the master answer): Legal doctrine that in certain cases an employer is liable for wrongful acts of employees.

Rest; rest the case: Said of an attorney who has completed presenting his or her case.

Retainer: Preliminary fee paid to an attorney; the act of obtaining the services of an attorney.

Rule nisi or **show cause:** Court order granted on a motion by either side to explain why what is sought cannot be granted.

Rule of court: Orders of and by a court; can be **special** if they pertain directly to the case being tried or **general** if they relate to court procedures for all cases.

Separation; sequestering: Refers to excluding witnesses from the courtroom until it is time to testify, except for the defendant and plaintiff.

Sine qua non (L., without which nothing): An indispenable factor, feature or condition.

Slander (L., **scandalum,** obstacle): Spoken defamatory remarks harmful to another's reputation or livelihood. (See also **Libel.**)

Stare decisis (L., to abide by): Legal doctrine that once a court has stated a principle on a point of law it will continue consistently to adhere to it in future similar cases.

Statute (L., **statutum,** law): Written legislatively enacted law.

Stay; To stop, hold or restrain; to suspend a case or part of it (**stay of proceedings**) and in so doing functions like an injunction; a **stay of execution** delays a prisoner's execution.

Stipulation (L., **stipulatus,** having spikes or stipules): Agreed conditions between attorneys such as incidental details of trial proceedings, acceptance of certain evidence or points of law, qualified expert witnesses, etc.

Subpoena (L., **sub poena,** under penalty): An order to appear in court at a specified date and time to give testimony (**subpoena ad testificandum**) or an order to produce or bring certain specified documents to trial (**subpoena duces tecum**).

Substantive law: Laws that create, define and regulate rights, duties and liabilities such as criminal, tort, contract, laws and the law of wills.

Summons (L., **summonee,** to remind secretly): A writ issued by a court to a named person officially notifying him or her that legal action has begun and listing the date and time to appear in court to answer the complaint.

Talesman (L., **tales de circumstantibus,** bystanders): A person summoned to serve as juror from among the bystanders in the courtroom.

Testimony (L., **testimonium,** that which is testified): Evidence by a competent witness under oath. While **testimony** and **evidence** are often used interchangeably, testimony is only such evidence as is spoken or written by a witness.

Tort (L., **tortus,** twisted): A wrongful act by direct violation of another's rights or neglect of public or private duty or obligation which caused damage or injury. There are three necessary elements for tort action: a legal duty binding on the defendant to the plaintiff, a breach of that duty, the breach being the proximate cause of the dȧmage or injury to the plaintiff.

Transcript (L., **transcriptus,** copy): Copy of the verbatim record of a trial or hearing.

Transitory: Term used to describe actions which can occur anywhere; they are termed **local** if they occur only in a specific location.

Traverse (L., **traversare,** to cross): To deny, such as the plaintiff's declaration in civil cases or the indictment in criminal cases.

Trial (French, **trier,** to try): A formal judicial examination and determination of issues of law and fact, civil or criminal, between two parties. (See also **Nisi pruis.**) A **trial de novo** is a new trial or a retrial in a higher court and the entire case is argued again as if for the first time.

Undue influence: Legal doctrine referring to influence on a person which weakens free will or any improper or wrongful constraint on a person, the effect of which is to conform that person's will to that of another (e.g. taking advantage of a person's weaknesses or when in need).

Venire (L., **venire facias,** jury panel): List of jurors summoned for a term; jurors are **veniremen;** when a new jury is needed it is **venire facias de novo;** when attorneys select from among the jurors it is **voir dire.**

Venue (L., **venire,** to come): The court jurisdiction in which damage or injury occurred. If it can be shown that media publicity or widespread public opinion would be likely to prejudice the court or jury, a **change of venue** is requested.

Verdict (L., **veredictum,** true declaration): The formal decision or finding of the jury.

Vicarious liability: Legal doctrine that an organization or institution is liable for the wrongful acts of others (e.g. business firms, hospitals, school systems, etc.).

Waiver of immunity: When a witness renounces the Fifth Amendment right protecting against self-incrimination.

Wanton: Reckless disregard of consequences and the safety and welfare of others; malicious or immoral acts; undisciplined, unruly, unjustified acts.

Weight of evidence (See **Proof**).

Willful: Voluntary intent, not carelessly or inadvertently.

Witness (Old English, **witnes,** witness): One who personally observes something then testifies to it under oath. (See also **Expert witness.**)

Writ (Old English, **writan,** to write): Court order requiring performance of a specified act.

Wrongful death; wrongful life: Suit brought to recover monetary damages for the **wrongful death** of a person due to negligence or for **wrongful life** such as when there have been unsuccessful sterilization, tubal ligations or vasectomies.

GLOSSARY REFERENCES

American Bar Association (1980). *Law and the courts.* Chicago, IL: Author.
Black, H. C. (Ed.) (1979). *Black's law dictionary.* St. Paul, MN: West Publishing.
Mish, F. C. (Ed.) (1983). *Webster's ninth new collegiate dictionary.* Springfield, MA: Merriam-Webster, Inc.

NOTE: All of the foregoing definitions were written by the author especially for this book in an effort to describe them in clear and understandable terms for nonlawyers. The above references were used to ensure accuracy.

AUTHOR INDEX

A

Aceves, 17
Adams, 27-28, 73
Addison, 47
Adler, 18, 91-92
Amiel, 53
Appleman, 40
Aquinas, 18
Aristotle, 21-22, 54
Augustine, 20

B

Bartlett, 91, 94
Bartol, 92
Beecher, 29
Black, 160
Boycott, 129
Braude, 57, 94
Bryan, 34
Buddha, 19
Buescher, 54, 57
Burke, 27
Butler, 94

C

Caesar, Julius, 24
Cataline, 24, 57
Catlin, 30
Cavett, 57
Chamberlin, 20
Christie, 34
Chu, 88-89, 109
Cicero, 6, 24, 71, 73-74
Claudius I, 46-47
Clay, 28-29
Clemens, 46, 58
Commins, 21, 25, 27
Cooper, 56
Cromwell, 63
Curiae, 58-59

D

Daniels, 75, 80, 89, 90
Darrow, 36, 48, 57
Dershowitz, 64-67
Dostoevski, 53
Draco, 148
Dryden, 27
Dunne, 47

E

Edwards, 3
Eliot, 21, 48
Emerson, 34, 56, 91, 99, 103, 119

F

Feldman, 20
France, 45-46, 59
Franklin, 28

G

Graves, 46

H

Hammurabi, 19
Hastie, 51
Henry VIII, 25
Hess, 6
Hobbes, 25
Holmes, 29, 30
Homer, 19
Hughes, 91, 93

I

Ibsen, 56-57
Inge, 19
Inker, 75, 78, 80-81

J

James, 52
Jay, 28
Jefferson, 18, 28, 57, 91
Jesus, 8
Jonson, 57
Joubet, 56

K

Kant, 26-27
Keeton, 64
Kester, 3, 60
King, 17
King John, 24-25
Krafte, 75
Kramer, 19
Kurke, 52

L

Lamsa, 91
Leavens, 49
Lincoln, 67-72
Linscott, 21, 25, 27
Locke, 18, 25-26
Lowenthal, 45
Luther, 20

M

Mann, 30
MacHovec, 54, 120
Marcus Aurelius, 23-24
Mark Anthony, 24
Marshall, 28
McCoid, 83-86, 89-90
Medina, 13
Mencken, 34, 45, 94
Mill, 8, 49, 95
Milton, 25
Mish, 33, 160
Momjian, 75, 76-77, 81-82
Monahan, 94
Montaigne, 33, 45, 57, 59
Morgan, 3, 4
Moses, 20

O

Old Testament, 19
Ostroff, 7, 74-75, 86, 87, 94, 118

P

Peale, 64
Penn, 57
Pierce, 92-93
Plato, 21-22, 48
Plutarch, 23, 45
Psalms, 20

R

Raleigh, 46
Reed, 34
Rogers, 51, 56
Rousseau, 27

S

Saks, 51
Sandburg, 57, 58, 61, 67-72
Shakespeare, 25, 49, 100
Socrates, 48, 54, 94
Stafford, 71
St. Paul, 91
Socrates, 8, 21, 22, 48
Solomon, 20-21
Solon, 23
Sophocles, 22-23
Sullivan, 60
Swift, 26, 48

T

Tennyson, 53
Truman, 29-30
Twain, Mark, 46, 58

V

Virgil, 3
Voltaire, 27

W

Walkes, 94
Webb, 8, 30, 95
Wesley, 119
Whitehead, 48

SUBJECT INDEX

A

Abandon, abandonment, 121
Academy, Plato's 21
Actionable, 13, 122
Actus rea, 12, 122
Adequate care, 122
Ad hominem (personal) attacks, 64, 74, 118, 123
Adjective law, 11
Administrative law, 11
 judge, 123
Adversary system, 7, 8, 33-34, 48, 49, 51, 56, 71, 95, 123
Adverse witness, 123
Agreement with other experts, 94
Algorithms, as trial tactic, 53
American Digest System, 96
American history, law in, 27
Ancient civilizations, law in, 17, 18-19
Anglo-Saxon legal tradition, 30
Answer, 14, 125
Antigone, 22
A priori deduction, 93, 126
Appeals courts (*see* Courts)
Appeals, filing, 47
Appearance, physical, 78
Arabic (Islamic) law, 19
Aristotle, on law, 22, 54
Arraign, arraignment, 15, 126
Arrest warrant, 14
Art or science tactic, 115
Assumption of risk, 126
Attorney, 122 (*see also,* Lawyer)
Attractive nuisance doctrine, 127
Average person test, 127
Award, 12, 127

B

Badges of fraud, 128
Bail bond, 14
Bailiff, 35, 128
Battery, 128
Bedfellow-type lawyer, 64
Belittling, needling, 112
Best defense lawyer (Dershowitz), 66-67
Best evidence, 128
Beyond a reasonable doubt, 93, 129
Bind over, bound over, 15, 129
Borrowed servant/worker doctrine, 129
Brain dead, 129
Breach of contract, of care, 130
Brevity, 46-47
Brief, 35, 130
Brown v State, 5
Burden of proof, of persuasion, 130
"But for" test, 130

C

Capital crime, 12
Captain of the ship doctrine, 130
Care, standard of, reasonable, slight, great, 131
Case law, 5, 11, 131
Cast, of courtroom drama, 35
Cause, probable, proximate, reasonable, 131
Centering, 101
Character assassination, 74, 118
Characterization, 133
Charter of Liberties, 25
Chilling effect doctrine, 133
China, 19
Church and state, 19
Circumstantial evidence, 133
Civil commitment, 134

Civil law, 12
 civil rules, 13
Civil statutes, 10-11
Claims courts (see courts)
Claims-made policy, 134
Clark v Pennsylvania Railroad, 13
Claymont v School District, 5
Clear and convincing, 134
Clear and present danger, 134
Closing argument, 44, 135
Clothing, appropriate for court, 100
Color of law, colorable transactions, 135
Common Law, 11, 135
 Antigone and, 22
 problem with, 13
Communications gap, lawyer-expert, 52
Competence, 11-12, 136
Complaint, 13, 38
Computer databases, legal, 96
Confidentiality, 137
Conflicting testimony, 90
Consent, express, implied, informed, 137
Consistency with other experts, 94
Constitution, 9, 10, 28, 138
Constitutional law, 11, 138
 John Marshall on, 28
Consulting experience, 78
Contempt of court, direct, indirect, 138
Controlled substance, 12
Court as drama, 34
Court chronology, sequence of events, 36
Court law, 11
Court order, 88
Courtroom decor, furnishings, 34
Courts, types of: federal, 9-10
 state, 10
 differences, 10
Credibility, 76, 79, 141
 credibility checklist, 79-80
Credibily informed, 141
Criminal insanity, 141
Criminal law, 12, 141
 criminal rules, 13
Criminal statutes, 10-11
Critique of Practical Reason, 26
Critique of Pure Reason, 26
Cross-complaint, cross-action, 14, 142
Cross examination, 42, 142
Cruel and inhuman, 142
Cruel and unusual, 142
Custom and usage, 142
Customs court (*see* Courts)

D

Damage suits, 4
 damages, 142-143
Danger to self or others, 12
Danger invites rescue doctrine, 143
Declaration of Independence, law and, 18
Deep pockets, 4, 144
Defendant, defense, 12-13, 144
Deposition, 14, 38, 84, 145
Depraved mind, 145
Diligent inquiry, 146
Diminished capacity doctrine, 146
Direct attack, 111, 146
Direct examination, 40, 147
Discoverability, 37, 82-83, 88-90, 94, 147
Discovered peril doctrine, 147
Dismissal without prejudice, 148
District courts (*see* Courts)
Doom's Day defense, 111
Dress, for court, 100
Drinking, 102
Drugs, use of, 102
Due process, 148

E

Education and training, 76
Emperor Claudius I, as a judge, 46
Employment history, 76
Engagement letter (lawyer-expert), 87
European history, law in, 24
Evasive, don't be, 108
"Ever make mistakes" tactic, 116
Experience, in court, 77
Experience, years of, 77
Exception, argument by, as a tactic, 53, 54
  (*see also* p. 149)
Expert consultant, 37
Expert witness, 37
 as idea and ideal, 8, 91-92
 as "battle of wits", 8
 "boom" industry, 3
 in case law, 5
 consulting, 78
 credibility, 76
 definitions, 4-5
 diplomates, 7-8
 duties, 6, 8
 education and training, 76

employment history, 76
engagement letter, 87
experience, 77
in history, 8
honors, awards, 78
initial lawyer contact, 86
licenses, certification, 77
memberships, leadership, 78
mental prep, 78
oath, 6
physical prep, 78
publications, citations, 77
selecting experts, 67
sources of, 5
teaching presentations, 77
testimony scope, depth, 5
varieties of, 6
virtues of, 76
who are they, 4
Eye contact, 102
Eyewitness testimony, unrealiability of, 46

F

Facial expression, 103
Fact witness, 5-6
Fair preponderance, 149
Federal court system, 9-10
Federal Register, 96
Federal rules of evidence, 4-5, 6-7
Federal Supplement, 96
Felony, 12, 14, 149
Fines in ancient law, 19
Freud, 22
Frivolous lawsuits, 4
Frye v United States, 7
Full-time experts, 74

G

Gestures, 102
Golden Rule, law and, 18
Grand jury, 14
Gratuitous guest doctrine, 156
Great Books of the Western World, 18
Greek chorus, as conscience, 22
Greek legal heritage, 21
Greek morality plays, 22
Grounding, 101
Guardian ad litem, 150
Gulliver's Travels, 26

H

Half-lie tactic, 53
Half-truth tactic, 53
Hammurabi, code of, 19
Hearsay, 150
Hebraic law, 20
Henry VIII, 25
Higher law, appeal to, 23
Hired gun or village blacksmith, 74
Honors, awards, distinctions, 78
Hostile witness, 150
Hypothetical questions, coping with, 109

I

"I don't know," using, 107
"If-then" shaping tactic, 111
"Iffy" questions, 108
Iliad, Homer's, 19
Impeach you, 42
India, karmic law, 19
Indictment, grand jury, 13-14, 150
Information, prosecutor's, 14
Initial contact with lawyer, 86
Injunctive relief, 12, 151
Injury, 4
Inquisition, Spanish, 19
Insanity, 11-12
Instructing the jury, 44, 151
Integrity-type lawyer, 66
Intent, 29
Interrogatories, 14, 38, 83, 84, 151
Islamic law, 19

J

Jargon, 102, 107
Jesus, trial of, 8
Jewelry, in court, 100
Jews, law of, 20
Judge, 34, 58, 80
Judge's law, 11
Jury system, origin, 19, 23
forming opinion, 40, 42, 47
Justice, 17-31

K

Karma, karmic law, 19
Kim v Superior Metals, 5
Knowing, four ways of, 92
Knowledge, opinion, truth contrasted, 92

L

Law, as idea and ideal, 17-31
 and psychology, 52
 and science, 52-53
 and tradition, 18
 types of, 10-12
Law library, how to use, 95
Law of Karma, 19
Laws, Plato's, 21
Lawsuits, number of, 3
Lawyers, in history, 58
 number of, 59-60
 types of, 60
Lawyer jokes,56-58
Layer cake tactic, 110
Leading questions, 110 (*see also* p. 151)
Leading the witness, 41-43
Learned treatise, 93, 114
Legal realities, historical, 45
Letters rogatory, 151
Leviathan, 25
Libel, 152
Licenses, certification, 77
Lincoln, as lawyer, 67-72

M

Magna Carta, 24-25
Malpractice suits, 3, 5, 6, 36, 57
 number of, 3-4
Mannerisms, 78
Material evidence, materiality, 93, 152
Matters at issue, 14
McCulloch v Maryland, 28
Media-oriented lawyer, 65
Meditations (Marcus Aurelius), 23-24
Memberships, leadership, 78
Mental anguish, mental cruelty, 152
Mental disorder, 11-12, 152-153
Mental health law, 11-12
Mental preparation for court, 104-106
Mens rea, 12, 152
Microphone, using, 103
Misdemeanor, 12, 153
Morality plays, 22
Moral law, 17-31
Motions: to dismiss, 13
 make certain, 13
 quash, 13
 strike, 13
 directed verdict, new trial, 153
Movies of trial procedures, 36

N

Natural law, 17-31
Negligence, 153-154
Nervous mannerisms, 102
Nitpicking technique, 54
Nolo contendere, 13, 154
Normal, what it is, 52
Not guilty plea, 8, 13 (*see also* Non compos mentis, 154)

O

Objection, 41, 154 (*see also Exception, 149)*
Occurence policy, 154
Odyssey, Homer's 19
Oedipus Rex, 22
Ole Philosopher type lawyer, 63
Ole Yeller type lawyer, 61
Opening statement, 40, 154
Opinion and truth, 92
Overanswering, 94, 109
Overzealous lawyer, 66

P

Pace yourself (take your time), 108
Pacing, "the pacer" tactic, 114
Party, 13, 154
Patent courts (*see* Courts)
Pause that refreshes, using, 108
Peremptory challenge, 155
Perjury, 41, 155
Perry Mason type lawyer, 65
Petition, 38, 155
Physical or mental exam, order for, 85
Physical preparation for court, 100-104
Physical traits, appearance, mannerisms, 78
Plaintiff, 12, 13, 155
Planning, 106
Plato, on law, 21, 48
Plea bargaining, 15, 155
Pleadings, 13, 38, 155
Points of law, 14
Posture, 101
Praecipe for sumons, 13, 38, 155
Precedent, 11, 13, 29, 93, 155
Preliminary hearing, 15
Preponderance of evidence, 93, 155
Pretrial conference, 14, 38
Pretrial phase, 36

Preventing panic, 102
Primary evidence, 128
Privilege, privileged communication, 156
Probable cause, 156
Procedural law, 11-12
Production for inspection, 85
Proof, legal, 93, 156
Proximate cause, 156
Psalms, psalter, and law, 20
Psychic harm, 5
Psychosis, 12
Publications, citations, 77
"Published?" tactic, 115

Q

Qualifying, 40, 41, 80-92

R

Rapid-fire questions, 113 (*see also* Speedy Gonzalez)
Realities, legal, historical, 45
Reasonable doubt, 156
Rebuttal evidence, 44, 156
Recognizance, on your own, 15
Recross examination, 44
Redirect examinations, 43, 157
Regional Reports, 96
Reincarnation, as rehabilitation, 19
Relevant evidence, 93
Religion and law, 19
Remanded, 15
Reply, 14, 157
Republic, Plato's, 21
Request for admission, 85
Rousseau's social contract, 27
Rules of Civil Procedure, 11

S

Salem witch trials, 19
Sarcasm, coping with, 112
Scientific method, 93
Selecting expert witnesses, 75-82
Semantics, 100
Sequestered, being, 50, 82, 157
Settlement, 12
Sexism tactic, 115
Shakespeare, on higher truths, 25
Shaping truth, 53
Similar cases attack, 115
Slang, 102, 107
Social conformity, 19
Social contract (Rousseau), 27
Socrates, trial of, 8, 21, 48, 54, 94
Sophocles, 22
Spanish Inquisition, 19
Special grand jury, 14
Specialized vocabulary, 102, 107
Speedy Gonzalez type lawyer, 62
Standard of care, 131
Stare decisis doctrine, 157
State court system, 10
State reports, 96
Statutory law, 10-11, 157
Stipulations, 14, 39, 158
Streetfighter-type lawyer, 64
Subpoena, 39, 158
 types of, content, 87
Substantive law, 10-11
Sumer, law in, 19
Summation, 44
Sumons, 158
Supreme Court Reports, 96
Surgeon-type lawyer, 60
Surprise witness, 44
Surrebuttal, 44
Swearing in, 41
Sweetheart-type lawyer, 62

T

Teaching experience, presentations, 77
Technical terms, 102, 107
Ten Commandments, 20
Theocracy, 19
Theoretical bias tactic, 115
Trial phase sequence of events, 39 (*see also* Pretrial phase, 36)
Trial procedures, 13-15, 37-44
Truth, nature of, 17-31, 48, 56, 93-95

U

Underanswering, 94
Undue influence doctrine, 159
Unfamiliar data, coping with, 108
Universal Declaration of Human Rights, 29
Ur-Nammu tablets (Sumerian), 19
Using a law library, 95
U. S. Supreme Court, 9-10

V

Verdict, 44, 159
Virtues of Ideal expert, 76
Voice, tone, volume, 101

W

Weight of evidence, 100 (*see also* Proof, 156)
"Whatcha got there" tactic, 113
"What if" questions, 109
"What you read biased you" tactic, 116
Witch trials, 19
Witness registries, 7
Words in your mouth, avoiding, 108
Word world, law as, 7, 54, 100
Worst case scenario defense, 111
Worst defense lawyer (Dershowitz), 66-67
Wrongful death, wrongful life, 189

Y

Yes-no tracking tactic, 110
Yoga, 22
"You be the judge" tactic, 114
"Your opinion was bought" tactic, 116
"Your X is not good enough" tactic, 117
"You were too superficial" tactic, 116

QUICK REFERENCE INDEX

ATTITUDE AND BEHAVIOR REVIEW

A

Appearance, 78
Arrange notes, materials, 102-103
Attitude, 118

C

Centering, grounding, 101
Clothing, jewelry, 100

D

Drinking, drugs (don't!), 102

E

Evasive (don't be), 108
Eye contact, optimal, when to avoid, 102

F

Facial expression, 103
Focus, fix on main points, 107

G

Gestures, 102

I

"I don't know" is OK, 107

J

Jargon, technical terms, 102, 107

M

Mannerisms, 78, 102
Mental prep (reread as therapy), 104-106
Microphone, using, 103

P

Pacing, pausing, taking your time, 108
Physical prep (reread as therapy), 100-104
Planning (relieves tension), 73, 106
Posture, 101
Prevent panic, 102

R

Review notes, materials, 107

V

Voice quality, 101

W

Word economy, don't overanswer, 109

QUICK REFERENCE INDEX

COPING IN COURT

A

Agreement, consistency with other experts, 90, 94
Algorithm system (of opposing attorney), 53
A priori deductive reasoning, 93, 126
"Art or science? Which is your field/ testimony?", 115

B

Badgering, belittling, needling, 61-62, 112
Bias, being accused of, 115, 116

C

Conflicting testimony (same as Agreement, above)
Consistency, your pretrial and trial testimony, 55

D

Direct attack, getting "nuked", 61-62, 111
Doom's Day defense (yours), 111

E

"Ever make a mistake? Making one now?", 116
Exception-becomes-the-rule technique, 54

H

Half-lie, half-truth, 53
Homey or humorous opposing attorney, 63-64
Hypothetical questions, "what if . . ," 105, 109

I

"If . . . then . . . " What could change your opinion?, 111
"Iffy" unclear questions, 108

L

Layer cake multi-level questions, 100
Leading or loaded questions, stacked deck, 42-43, 110
Learned treatise, 93, 114

N

Nitpicking, trivial pursuit, 54

P

Pacer-walker opposing attorney, 114
Personal (ad hominem) attack, 64
"Published (like my expert)?", 115

R

Rapid-fire questions, 62, 113

S

Sarcasm by opposing attorney, 62
Seductive opposing attorney, real charmer, 62
"Seen similar cases? Didn't think so!", 115
Sexist put-downs, 115

U

Unfamiliar data, surprised with, 108

W

"Whatcha got in front of you there?", 113
Wooden leg: "Your ___ isn't good enough," 117
Words-in-your-mouth technique, 108

Y

Yes-no tracking, 54, 108
"You be the judge" trap, 114
"Your opinion was bought, paid for," 111
"You were/are superficial, ineffectual," 116

(Anticipate *lawyer types*, 60-67)